LIVE, LAUGH, & LOVE

8 LIFE-CHANGING STRATEGIES TO HELP YOU

LIVE WELL, LIVE BLESSED!

This book is dedicated to Irene Johnson Patterson and Danielle Frank-Lemon.
May you rest in Heaven; I miss you so much!

CYNTHIA A. PATTERSON

LIVE, LAUGH, & LOVE

8 LIFE-CHANGING STRATEGIES TO HELP YOU LIVE WELL, LIVE BLESSED!

Seeds of Love Publishing
Discovering your voice to share your story
HOUSTON

CONTENTS

LIFE REFLECTION

This passage of scripture resonated with me several years ago: "Daughter, you took a risk of faith, and now you're healed and whole. Live well, live blessed! Be healed of your plague (Mark 5:34, MSG)." The key words that literally leaped off the pages were "Live well, live blessed!" As a result, I have been on a mission to experience this blessed life on my journey and to help other women as well. As I reflect on the past chapters of my life, it helped me to realize, I must effectively serve women by using discernment, wisdom, and the Holy Spirit. This knowledge shaped my beliefs to understand I am here as a servant of God to minister to the heart of women that will cause authentic transformation. Admittingly, there were many do-overs, heartbreaks, disappointments, that would generally make a person want to give up and admit defeat. However, I found it as a motivation and very intriguing to see what the end would be. For the population I work with, to see how God has literally turned my mess into a ministry, has been the most rewarding. I am honored to receive the assignment to work with women that have issues of drug and alcohol substance abuse, depression, PTSD, sexual assault, domestic violence, anxiety, low self-esteem, and self-defeating beliefs (i.e. I'm not worthy; I can't do anything right). To sit across from these women and look into sad eyes, (eyes which reveal the depth of the soul) and ask questions to help me understand what she is going through is rewarding and a blessing. For instance, I might ask: "How would you let go and move forward?" This is not a difficult question, but it is asked to help each woman understand the hardest lessons learned can be the simplest if we listen (Patterson, 2015)"[1]. Beginning the question with "how" states in what manner or by what means does she plan to let go and move forward. Sounds easy right? But for some it is very complex.

Through this journey, I've learned God has bestowed me with the spiritual gift of discernment. I can tell when I am doing too much; because, I am off in what Calhoun says:

"Discerning the problems of the spiritual life, discernment is frequently needed in personal growth. The moment we begin to take our life with God seriously, we begin to encounter problems. A failure to understand this process hassled some to experience severe setbacks. It has to do with our whole attitude toward God and ourselves, with an ongoing relationship with God and loving him." (Calhoun, 2005)[2]

As a transformation life coach, I must understand I cannot allow the enemy to dupe the women that come into my space. Writing this guidebook has challenged me to look introspectively at my own spiritual disciplines and be intentional concerning taking the exercises, discussions, personal journaling, and other tasks seriously. It also helped me to understand that I need to stay within the scope of my ability of experience and training for now. The American Counseling Associations states, "Counselors practice only within the boundaries of their competence, based on their education, training, supervised experience, state and national professional credentials, and appropriate professional experience (ACA, 2014, Sec C.2.a.)" [3]. In other words, I must be intentional to *"stay in my lane."* Staying in my lane translates into having no competition; because, I am in my own lane. What I mean by that is simply this: it's so easy to get distracted - distracted from your vision, distracted from your values, distracted from your focus when you're measuring your success and your performance by what others are doing.

Personally, I have been involved in extensive education and training to become an expert in my own area of specialty in what

I am doing as a transformation life coach. I believe coaches must be competent and work within the scope of how they have been trained. It is important for us to know the current information impacting our profession. Staying abreast of new ideas and new information can assist us in providing great success strategies and holistic approaches that our clients need. It also helps us in the field of emotional healing and wellness; because, this field details so many transformations that a woman should go through. We must be equipped for what I call those *"blind spots"* that come during our journey together, and if I am not equipped, it could cause harm to a woman that I am purposed to help.

Honestly, this guidebook was a spiritual awakening for me. The reality is I cannot equip anyone if I am stale and empty. This guidebook helped me to see 1) Self-Care is very important. Balance and self-care were the keys to my success in completing this book project. I took advantage of the time in preparation of this resource to go deep, and allow God to eliminate dryness and emptiness, which most of my co-laborers often shared they were feeling as well. God's word says to "ask and it shall be given unto me" (Matthew 7:7, KJV). Through these years, there was a common thread woven together, and it was prayer. Prayer has become my lifeline to Heaven. I believe the greater the prayer, the greater the faith. It becomes the oxygen for my daily living. It goes ahead of me and takes care of everything that concerns me. Therefore, I must make prayer a rule for life. This rule will help me not only survive, but to thrive. In her book *The Intercessors Handbook*, Jennifer Eivaz encourages us to understand that: "Prayer is like breathing. It becomes oxygen to our spirit. When we pray, we feel alive and connected to God." 2) Setting healthy boundaries in relationships is important to maintaining them. Research has proven that people who feel connected to others live longer, healthier lives. Creating and maintaining healthy relationships is essential to our well-being, yet not always easy. Sometimes we have to set boundaries with people, which can be hard to do (I'm sure this makes sense especially if you relate to being a people-pleaser). What exactly are healthy boundaries? When do we set them? How do we do it in a way that is loving? These are the questions, I plan to explore with you in this guidebook. I also reveal the number one reason why so many of us know we should set a boundary with someone, but we do not follow through with it. We are all in a season to learn and grow, so it's natural to experience growing pains with people you care about. The key word here is "growing" not "pain." Setting boundaries is part of growth. In almost every area of my life, I must have healthy boundaries. Healthy boundaries establish a sense of trust and security between self, family, friends, mentees, and clients. They help us to stay on track, and they keep us from making errors that will harm us. 3) I decided to develop new disciplines to hold me accountable. Oprah Winfrey has been quoted as saying: "Surround yourself only with people who are going to take you higher." I can't even begin to tell you how important it is to have the right people with you. Often, I say you must have the right "tribe" that has your back. Your "tribe" are the women that just 'get' you; They understand. They will share in your interests. They will cheer you on when you succeed and commiserate with you in your failures. Your tribe will accept you for who you are. They will be your support system, your cheering squad, and will provide you with a sense of community that you will be hard-pressed to find elsewhere. 4) Being a caregiver for my mother while she battled stage IV breast cancer taught me to walk in humility. Walking in humility strips me of pride and shows that I am not independent of God. I know that makes God smile; because, He will not share his glory with anyone else. Seeking God gives Him more reason to allow me to live in peace and live more abundantly. Lastly, 5) Being more spiritually mature helped me become a healthier woman with sharp wisdom and keen discernment. This will help me to become more Christ-minded.

Throughout this guidebook there are many exercises for you to do, wisdom notes for you to read, and things for you to remember. We will explore the very root of which your issue stems from and the process in healing, including: what we know about healing itself, what causes the emotions which drive us, and how our brain's control system is hard-wired to them. For each of these thoughts, I have developed symbols to help guide you through the process. So, please understand it is going to take work. You must work out your own salvation (Philippians 2:12). It is about changing your mind set and allowing yourself to (Romans 12:2-3) to live, laugh, and love. You are in a new chapter now, and you can write this chapter however you deem to write it. I made the choice, and I can truly say that I believe I am a better mother, better grandmother, better mentor, better friend, and better entrepreneur because of the development of this guidebook. I cannot just limit my reflection to the guidebook. I have had a spiritual awakening living well and living a blessed life. I know I am forever growing. As the cliché says, I am not where I want to be, but thank God, I am not where I used to be. In this next chapter of my life, I must be open to reorganize and adjust without compromising who I am. I am praying even now to God, that you broaden your mind to the possibility of Him using you too. Although it will be a slow and painful process at times, just know you will make it through all those times as well. As we all know, life happens and there are times when the unexpected happens. God has allowed me to work outside my comfort zone to do the extraordinary. I am excited for you too. Now, let's get started, and it begins by determining what's important.

STRATEGY ONE
FOCUS ON WHAT'S IMPORTANT

L IFE CAN BE LOUD.
Often it can seem like we are busily chugging through life, weighed down by an unending list of to-dos, and an ever-growing list of not-yet-dones. We live in a society that thrives on busyness. Fast-food drive-thrus, microwaves, supercenters, and the growing demand for online and televised church services are only a few by-products of our need-it-now culture. And lately, I've noticed that every moment gained by utilizing my time-saving device is quickly filled with another task. The mental and emotional capacity required to successfully complete, or even attempt the goals we have set, can leave us feeling like we are living out the latest zombie movie as one of the title characters – zoned out, hungry, tripping over our feet, falling apart, and overflowing with all the wrong emotions.

God used the story of two well-known women in the Bible to demonstrate to us the type of relationship He wants with each of us. In Luke 10:38-42 (NIV):

> 38 As Jesus and his disciples were on their way, he came to a village where a woman named Martha opened her home to him. 39 She had a sister called Mary, who sat at the Lord's feet listening to what he said. 40 But Martha was distracted by all the preparations that had to be made. She came to him and asked, "Lord, don't you care that my sister has left me to do the work by myself? Tell her to help

me!" 41 "Martha, Martha," the Lord answered, "you are worried and upset about many things, 42 but few things are needed—or indeed only one. Mary has chosen what is better, and it will not be taken away from her."

When I read these scriptures, I get the image of a house busy with people engaged in numerous conversations around the house. It must have been a huge house to hold as many people as it did. In my research, the age of Martha and Mary was not determined. But it was estimated that they may have been around and about Jesus' age. Therefore, if we would fast forward to the 21st century, they would be millennial women between the ages 18-34. Somewhere in a secluded corner, the Lord Jesus Christ is calmly teaching a handful of people who are intently listening to His every word. Mary is sitting at His feet, very content and very settled. Scripture says that Martha is running about trying to figure out how everybody is going to get fed and coordinating the planning of cooking for all the people.

I can imagine Martha texting Mary "Hey sis, come to the kitchen and help me." "Hello sis, are you coming?" "Hey sis, where are you? I need you to come and help?" "Hello?!" "Okay ...really?!" Come into the kitchen NOW!!! Martha blowing up her phone. However, Mary's phone is in her bedroom just buzzing and chiming away. Martha thought about it and concluded "she does not have her phone"; therefore, she frantically rushes over to interrupt the intimate gathering. Picture this, everyone casually looks up at her as the Lord easily sets the record straight. Feeling compassion for Martha, Jesus says to her "Martha Martha you are worried and upset about many things, but few things are needed—or indeed only one. Mary has chosen what is better, and it will not be taken away from her."

Sometimes we just forget how big our God is, and we run around like Martha trying to make everything just right. All we need to do in these moments is to just "Trust in the Lord with all our heart; and lean not unto our own understanding, acknowledge God, and he will direct our path (Proverbs 3:5-6)." Jesus told us to "seek first the Kingdom of God, and his righteousness and all these things will be added unto you (Matthew 6:33)." This is exactly what Mary did. She sought Jesus first.

Whereas, Martha was concerned about "what shall we eat, what shall we drink."

Life can be loud and in the midst of the noise, God's voice can get drowned out. What can we learn from these sisters?

JESUS WILL MEET US WHERE WE ARE.

Luke 10:38 As Jesus and his disciples were on their way, he came to a village where a woman named Martha opened her home to him. We must discern when God is calling us. Do you have anything in the way that is blocking God's invitation? Martha immediately let Jesus in. She did not delay at all.

DISCERN WHAT SEASON YOU ARE IN.

Luke 10:39 She had a sister called Mary, who sat at the Lord's feet listening to what he said. Meaning Mary was still. Mary had a purpose. She realized life can be loud and she decided to not be moved by the noise not even her own family member. There comes a time where you are going to have to shut it all down. Give yourself permission to rest. One of my mentors have said these key words of wisdom, and at the time she said them, it liberated me: "You have to put yourself on your to do list." Likewise, I say this to you: place time spent with and for yourself on your agenda, on your calendar, in your planner, or whatever you call it. Self-care is so important. Refueling and renewing your mind, body, and spirit is imperative. The most magnificent thing about seeking to hear and understand the leading and will of God is if we seek Him, we will find Him (Jeremiah 29:12). That's a promise we can count on. "When you come looking for me, you'll find me. "Yes, when you get serious about finding me and want it more than anything else, I'll make sure you won't be disappointed (Jeremiah 29:13, The Message)."

BEWARE OF THE SUBTLE DISTRACTIONS.

Subtle distractions are those things that cause us to get frustrated and question God. Don't get the answers to your situation by looking within yourself but looking up to Jesus. It is illuminating to contrast Mary's reverence with Martha's demeanor. Martha was so comfortable with Jesus that she openly included Him in her frustration. Her words were found in Luke 10:40 "Lord, don't you care that my sister has left me to do the work by myself?" Can you hear the tone of her frustration? The more we think about our problems, the more complex the issues become.

Proverbs 23:7 says for as he thinketh in his heart, so is he. In other words, explore your feelings and your emotions by identifying those patterns of behavior that have you stuck. Dr. Dee C. Marshall wrote in her book *Get Out of Your Own Way*: When your outlook on life and emotional set-point defaults to negative that is self-sabotage.[5] There are 22 human emotions: 15 negative and 7 positive within each of those there are sub-emotions. Now, I challenge your thoughts. I challenge you to go deep within to discover what is distracting you. What do you focus on more?

Martha knew Jesus; because, she invited him in. Her priorities were more focused on the preparation than being with him. She lost focus on who Jesus was. Her thoughts and feelings became too self-focused. She turned her attention from Jesus and began watching Mary with a critical eye; which as a result ruined the whole evening for herself. Look what she said in the rest of verse 40: Tell her to help me!" She placed a demand on Jesus. Martha's behavior right here shows how subtly and sinfully human pride can corrupt even the best of our actions.

What Martha was doing was by no means a bad thing. She was waiting on Jesus and her guests. She was acting as a servant to all. She no doubt began with the best of motives and the noblest of intentions. But the moment she made something other than Jesus the focus of her heart and attention, her perspective became very self-centered. At that point, even her service to Christ became tainted with self-absorption and spoiled by a very uncharitable failure to assume the best of her sister. To you reading this, warning my dear; Please let me shout it loud and make it clear. Look deep within yourselves and don't be distracted by a multitude of thoughts; which has resulted into anger, resentment, jealousy, a critical spirit, judgment, and unkindness which will lead you into complaints. This leads to uneasiness and we will go ahead of God by doing things in our own will. I call this a destiny distractor. And it will distract you from making good Godly decisions. Tell yourself…

Let it Go. The reason you must let it go is; because, Jesus encourages us to! His conversation was in verse 41 "Martha, Martha," the Lord answered, "you are worried and upset about many things, verse 42 but few things are needed—or indeed only one.

Now replace your name with Martha…

"_____, _____" the Lord answered, "you are worried and upset about many things, but few things are needed—or indeed only one.

Question: What are you worried and upset about? Jesus is saying to you at this moment in time "only one thing is needed." It is your choice.

WE HAVE CHOICES IN LIFE.

Both women made a choice. Mary by contrast was so consumed with thoughts of Christ that she became completely oblivious to everything else. She sat at His feet and listened to Him intently, absorbing His every word. She was by no means lazy. She simply understood the true importance of this occasion. The son of God himself was a guest in her home. Listening to him and worshiping him were at that moment the very best use of Mary's energies and the one right place for her to focus her attention.

I don't know about you, but the thought of God saving me, God restoring me, God healing me, and the thought of his Son Jesus dying for me, makes me want to worship. My heart's desire is to give him praise and thanksgiving. "Mary has chosen what is better, and it will not be taken away from her." One thing that stood out about Mary of Bethany was her keen ability to observe and understand the heart of Jesus. Mary seemed to be able to discern Jesus' true meaning even better than any of the twelve disciples.

In John 12, her gesture of anointing Him in preparation for His burial at the beginning of that final week shows a remarkably mature understanding. That was the fruit of her willingness to sit, listen, and ponder. Because she chose what was better, it would not be taken away from her. What was better? It is the anointing that is better. She realized it is the anointing that destroys yokes. It's the anointing that when you are in your prayer closet and you think it has been 30 minutes and instead it has been two hours. It's the anointing that makes you feel you have a million dollars, but your bank account is in the negative. It will make you love your enemies. It will make you forgive. It will help you to develop a grateful attitude. It will help you to develop a peaceful and thankful heart (Colossians 3:15). Choosing what is better will last forever. His truth endures forever. The word of God will never fail us (Luke 1:37). That's why we must trust in His word. Being confident in this one thing: he who has begun a good work, shall complete it (Philippians 1:6). The Lord shall fight for you and you shall hold your peace (Exodus 14:14). He restores my soul; he leads me in the paths of righteousness for his name's sake (Psalm 23:3). You have turned for me my mourning into dancing (Psalm 30:11); Weeping may endure for a night, but joy comes in the morning (Psalm 30:5). These scriptures contain promises that we as women both in the role mentors or mentees should all hold dear.

If it is loud in your life right now, take this time to worship him. How do we do this? How do we begin to worship God? What does it take for us to develop the attitude of gratitude? Is there a practical application we can do to get us to the place of worship? To experience this peace God wants us to experience? Yes, there is. I am a firm believer that I must prepare for whatever I am about to embark upon. The following is a scripture that I stand on to confirm the conditions and promises of God:

Proverbs 21:5 The plans of the diligent lead surely to abundance, but everyone who is hasty comes only to poverty.

The following is a two-part exercise 1) **8-day Breakthrough & Meditation Worksheet** that will help you refocus on your worship and prayer in the morning to start your day; 2) **"Who Are You."** It is my prayer both parts will provide you wisdom and insight to get the most value of this guidebook. It is my role to coach and guide you to discover and turn your impossibilities to possibilities. Please be opened minded and objective to the possibility of being more equipped for the rest of the journey. For the next several days, these documents should be used to help you maximize the value of your participation and produce unprecedented results in your time with God.

8-DAY BREAKTHROUGH MEDITATION SCRIPTURES (MORNING MEDITATION AND WORSHIP)	
DAY 1	Focus: Clean Slate Meditation: Psalm 51:10; Psalm 32:5 Journal your thoughts by answering question(s): 1. *Is there something you might need to let go from yesterday in order to have a better today?*
DAY 2	Focus: Recommitment Meditation: Psalm 77:11-15 Journal your thoughts by answering question(s): 1. *What is one activity that needs to be dropped or toned down so that you can have more time for God? What would happen if you did an 180° on that?*
DAY 3	Focus: Forgive Yourself Meditation: Psalm 19:12-14 Journal your thoughts by answering question(s): 1. *Based on God's free forgiveness for you, what characteristics in your life might indicate that you haven't fully forgiven yourself, even if you know in your head what you need to do?*
DAY 4	Focus: Forgiving Others Meditation: Hebrews 8:12; Ephesians 4:21-32 Journal your thoughts by answering question(s): 1. *Is there a relationship in your life right now that has unresolved conflict and tension? Picture the person who has caused you the most hurt or the person who has greatly offended you. Imagine forgiving that person, and write down what that would look like.*
DAY 5	Focus: Loving Yourself Mediation: Psalm 139:13-18 Journal your thoughts by answering question(s): 1. *Since God delights in you because He loves you, how can you delight in how He created you?*
DAY 6	Focus: Self-Examination Meditation: Exodus 33:13; Psalm 86:11 Journal your thoughts by answering question(s): 1. *What actions or attitudes are keeping you from being the most attractive you can be for God?*
DAY 7	Focus: Accepting God's Love Meditation: Psalm 143:8-10 Journal your thoughts by answering question(s): 1. *What would be your first step in accepting God's love in your life in your current circumstance?*
DAY 8	Focus: Reflection and Acceptance Meditation: Romans 8:28 Journal your thoughts by answering question(s): 1. *What would you do different if you could live a part of your life over again?* 2. *What are some lessons God is currently teaching your through His Word in Romans 8:28 and through life lessons?*

PART 1

WHO ARE YOU
AN EXERCISE IN SELF-REFLECTION AND CHALLENGING ASSUMPTIONS.

Reflect on your life thus far and bring to mind some of the moments which helped to define who you are. Consider the following: Who are you? What is my ethnicity, my gender, my marital/partner status, my occupation, my interests, my accomplishments, my hopes, my dreams and my goals?

What do you strongly believe in? Who or what formulated these beliefs? How do I decide what is right vs. wrong?

List all of the groups or roles that you feel represent, influence and matter to you?	Of the groups/roles you identified, choose the five that are the most important to your perception of who you are.
	1.
	2.
	3.
	4.
	5.
	Use a pie chart to represent how those five groups/roles represent you.

PART 2

Now, look at your pie chart. This is how you see your life as of TODAY! Now, look at what you wrote down that is important to you and answer the following questions in your journal:

1. What's working for you? _____
    _____
    _____.

1. What's not working for you? _____
    _____
    _____.

2. Area(s) of your life you would like to work on? _____
    _____
    _____.

3. What's missing, what will make a difference in your life now?
    _____
    _____
    _____.

4. Based on your answer in #3, take what is missing and state it as a new possibility for it. Look up Gen.18:14, Luke 1:37_and in your own words, what do these scriptures mean to you and how would you apply them? _____
    _____
    _____.

5. Create your own affirmation as an encouragement to yourself.
    _____
    _____
    _____.

6. Write out your prayer to God in your own words. Date this prayer and thank Him in advance for your breakthrough.

_____

_____

_____

_____

_____.

   Now that you have completed the two exercises, you should have a better perspective of where to start with identifying challenges hindering you to live, laugh and love. As you continue this process, I ask for you to be open for the change God is doing on the inside of you. Take on the challenge of emerging in your spiritual growth and development.

STRATEGY TWO
TAKE ON THE CHALLENGE

A challenge is something new and difficult which requires great effort and determination. A challenge to something is a questioning of its truth or value. As we go through the process, we will discover emotional health is an important part of our overall wholeness. God wants us to "enjoy good health and that all may go well with us, even as our soul is getting along well (3 John 2)". It allows us to cope with life's challenges and enjoy life's pleasures. Being emotionally wounded can shift our perceptions of ourselves, our relationships, and the future in powerful ways. It may surprise you to know that statistically, the risk of emotional problems is highest. Any choice can bring upheavals in our lives, strong feelings, and difficulty coping.

I've coached many women who believe that it is impossible to be "traumatized," due to their understanding of what trauma is. At the end of our coaching session, they learn there are various kinds of experience that can be traumatic for a given person, including divorce, marriage, childbirth, job loss and more. Other examples of trauma include rape, physical abuse, severe illness, a war experience, an accident, natural disaster, or the death of someone close. This is important too: a person who has suffered previous trauma may have more difficulty handling any stressful experience.

If you think you have a history of unresolved trauma or have trouble coping in general, it may be even more important to get help from a counselor specializing in recovery from trauma. Also, if you have been diagnosed with depression, an anxiety disorder, addiction, or other mental health problems, please seek the help of your mental health professional. Not all women who experience something they think is bad feel traumatized. We don't fully understand what allows some women to get through an extremely stressful experience without trauma. We do know women who generally feel good about themselves, who feel support from those closest to them, and who can usually cope with stress, generally handle stressful experiences better. Jesus said to her, "Daughter, you took a *risk* of faith, and now you're healed and whole. Live well, live blessed! Be healed of your plague (Mark 5:34, MSG)." This word risk in Hebrew depicts of a woman brushing up against that moment when she knew that everything was at risk. It's the moment when she comes to the realization that what was most precious to her had to be left behind if she were to seek God first. There is an emptiness here. No, this emptiness is the gnawing certainty that her evaluation of life's priorities is about to be shattered. It is the uneasiness that there is a new dimension of spiritual connection waiting on the other side of total surrender, but she just can't see it. Right now, you feel you are alone in the dark. This could not be further from the truth. God is right there waiting for you to reach for Him, so you may be healed. But, it is you getting outside of your comfort zone. Not allowing the crowd or voices in your head to discourage you to not reach.

💭 WISDOM KEY APPLICATION

Risk factors include experiences like the following that may continue to trouble you:
• Domestic violence or abuse;
• Prior depression, anxiety disorder or other mental health problems;
• Previous trauma or impaired coping due to an earlier trauma;

- Opposition to a decision from someone close to you;
- Extreme lack of support, including the feeling (or reality) of no one to talk to;
- The ending of a relationship at the same time as a woman has an abortion;

Ideally, addressing these risk factors ahead of time would prevent the most severe reactions, but exploring these factors is certainly part of healing afterwards. We are complex. Our lives are complex. How we cope is a complex picture of our childhood, our life experiences, our self-definition and more. For example, if we focus on our abuse as the only cause of our problems, we miss the bigger picture. We might overlook things in our personal situation that can help us heal. This doesn't mean that your feelings are not real or even that you are in some way "wrong" if you are traumatized now. It means that to feel better you need to consider all the things that brought you to this point in your life. We must stop lying to ourselves as well as to others. We say we are okay, but really, we are not. According to the Apostle John, the Bible states "you say, 'I am rich. I have everything I want. I don't need a thing!' And you don't realize that you are wretched and miserable (Revelation 3:17)".

EXERCISE

WHAT ARE YOUR INTENTIONS OR GOALS?

I believe self-reflection begins with you. It is important to begin to challenge yourself. As a young girl, I was very competitive. I felt it was important to be my best. My parents put a high expectation on me to succeed. As a result, their expectations contributed to this attitude of over-achieving in everything I did; It somewhat turned me into a perfectionist. In the end, this need to over achieve caused disappointments within myself when things did not work out according to plan. So, one day, I asked myself a question: What are your intentions (goals)? Intention is a great word; because intention is an idea that you plan (or intend) to carry out. If you mean something, it's an intention. Your goal, purpose, and aim are a part of your intentions. It's something you mean to do, whether you pull it off or not. An example of specifically saying aloud what you want is when God asked Solomon in1 Kings 3:5, 10-13:

> *5 That night the Lord appeared to Solomon in a dream, and God said, "What do you want? Ask, and I will give it to you!" 10 The Lord was pleased that Solomon had asked for wisdom. 11 So God replied, "Because you have asked for wisdom in governing my people with justice and have not asked for a long life or wealth or the death of your enemies— 12 I will give you what you asked for! I will give you a wise and understanding heart such as no one else has had or ever will have! 13 And I will also give you what you did not ask for—riches and fame! No other king in all the world will be compared to you for the rest of your life! 14 And if you follow me and obey my decrees and my commands as your father, David, did, I will give you a long life."*

Therefore, let's get started by clarifying: saying aloud and writing down what healing will look like to you. Your intentions (goals) in doing this work may be to feel whole again. List your goals below. To help get you started, other women have said,

EXAMPLES:

"I want to feel good again. I want to stop hurting."
"I want to go to school and do well."
"I want to experience forgiveness."
"I want to feel at peace."
"I want to feel connected again to Jesus."
"I want to feel love again for my spouse."
"I want to feel normal again."

WHAT DO YOU WANT? (List as many as you like)

I want _____.

I want _____.

I want _____.

I want _____.

I want _____.

I want _____.

Are you ready to see an older and wiser version of you? I want to encourage you to take the lessons you've learned during the past years and strive to make the coming years your best. This is a time to make a choice about your life. You can learn and grow by developing a larger vision of yourself. When we face life's challenges with strength and courage, we become warriors and not worriers. It's a way to practice compassion and loving kindness toward yourself.

WRITE A PRAYER AND AFFIRMATION _____
_____
_____
_____.

In the meantime, spiritual growth and maturity is having discernment and wisdom. We must learn how to discern our feelings and not allow our emotions to hinder our progress.

STRATEGY THREE
GET OUT OF YOUR FEELINGS

WHY ARE YOU SO EMOTIONAL? This is a question my mother would ask me all the time. To illustrate the question, have you ever tried to put some water on a fresh wound? If you have tried, then you must have felt some pain. Water, which can never harm you if you were not injured, has just made you feel some pain when it touched your wound. In other words, when we develop a wound we tend to become over sensitive to factors that didn't use to bother us before. I came to realize one day while in prayer, the same goes for emotional wounds: What if you have some emotional wounds that are making you over-sensitive to factors that other people don't even notice? These small things that are bothering you may be harmless on their own, but yet they still hurt you. They touch your wounds just like the water did.

I need to make it clear that if you are going to truly heal, it is an absolute necessity that you identify and learn about emotional wounds and how together we will bring you to the point where you can receive inner healing from the Holy Spirit. The goal is not to forget a hurtful event or trauma, but to receive healing for that event, where the Holy Spirit removes the stinger from it. When we look back upon a healed wound, we can see it in a different way. It has been healed and is no longer painful to look back upon (Psalm 19:11, 139:23-24).

IDENTIFYING EMOTIONAL WOUNDS

Have you ever wondered why do you feel so bad when "he" didn't call you? Or when you are overlooked for a promotion by your boss? Have you ever thought why you were so crushed when your elementary music teacher said you could not sing? Or you were abandoned by your dad? Is it because that person is bad? Your wound in this case may be the need for social approval. You may have been wounded before by people who didn't approve of something about you, and now whenever someone ignores you again it hurts. It hurts not just because it should hurt, but because it touched your wound and reminded you of a past rejection.

There were times I found myself asking friends for reassurance about my looks just after breaking up with a guy? I would ask myself why am I experiencing so much pain? Did I love him that much? The answer to this question was often "no." It's just that I was wounded before and here that wound has been touched again. When I was young, people always used to make fun of me; because, I am dark skinned. Whenever someone rejected me, I felt bad, not because of the rejection, but because this rejection touched an old wound.

Why do you think a woman may feel broken and devastated when she gets a rejection letter? Is it because she really wanted the job that much? Not really. If she wanted it that much she would have felt bad about the rejection, but she wouldn't have felt broken. It's just that this rejection touched an old wound. When that woman was a child, her parents rarely used to encourage her and as a result she grew up lacking self-confidence in her abilities. Now whenever she gets a rejection letter she feels bad, not because of being worried about her future, but because of her old wound that hasn't yet healed.

Emotional wounds that haven't healed mean our thinking has become stuck, focused on a particular past life experience as permanent and inescapable. The wound itself is a perception of some event which has already happened and is dead, except that we keep it alive in our thoughts. The first thing we need to do is identify the problem and realize the need for inner healing. Below is a list of **common symptoms** to help you identify within yourself an emotional wound you may be experiencing:

Inner rawness: There's often a sense of inner rawness and hurt that doesn't seem to go away.

Irritability: It's easy to become irritable with others, even if they aren't doing anything wrong!

Little or no tolerance: There is a low tolerance issue with others, concerning what you expect and demand from them.

> **STOP AND JOURNAL** your thoughts by writing down which of the above emotions you are currently feeling and use this scripture to develop a prayer of mediation: **ROMANS 3:23 (NLT)** *"Don't judge others because you are no better than them For everyone has sinned; we all fall short of God's glorious standard."*

_____

_____

_____

_____

_____

_____

_____.

Negative feelings always rise up: Feelings of anger, hate, resentment, etc. seem to "rise up" within you at the slightest offense from others.

Overly sensitive about an event in your past: If there are events in your past which cause you to become very sensitive or angry, or even cause you to lash out, then it is likely revealing a deep emotional wound tied in with that event or memory.

Hard to forgive: it becomes very difficult, if not impossible to love and therefore forgive others. It can also be hard to forgive and love yourself. It can even be hard to forgive and love God, even though He has done nothing wrong against you!

Hard to feel loved: It is hard to clearly see and realize the love of others and God in your life. You may be surrounded by people who love you, but it can be difficult to fully feel and receive that love. There seems to be a wall up that blocks the flow of love into your life.

STOP AND JOURNAL your thoughts by writing down which of the above emotions you are currently feeling and use this scripture to develop a prayer of mediation: EPHESIANS 4:31-32 (NIV) *Get rid of all bitterness, rage and anger, brawling and slander, along with every form of malice. Be kind and compassionate to one another, forgiving each other, just as in Christ God forgave you.*

_____

_____

_____

_____

_____

_____

_____.

Lashing out: is when there's an inner wound that has festered, it becomes easy to lash out or have sudden outbursts of anger, hate, resentment, etc. You may find it easy to lash out at people who love you and have done you no harm.

Feeling of anger towards God: when a person has been wounded, it becomes easy to blame God for their troubles and hardships. This is the last thing that you want to do when seeking to be healed; because; this virtually puts a wall in your mind and heart that can block the healing power of the Holy Spirit to operate. Although He desires to heal your wound, He will not override your freewill, and if you hold hate in your heart against Him, it can block His efforts to heal your wounds.

> **STOP AND JOURNAL** your thoughts by writing down which of the above emotions you are currently feeling and use this scripture to develop a prayer of mediation: **PSALM 22:1–2 (NLT)** *My God, my God, why have you abandoned me? Why are you so far away when I groan for help? 2 Every day I call to you, my God, but you do not answer. Every night I lift my voice, but I find no relief.*

_____

_____

_____

_____

_____

_____

_____.

Self-hate: Many times, when a person is hurt from past abuse; they will begin to think that perhaps what happened to them was deserved because of something they did or the way that they were. This is not true. Abuse is never acceptable, even if a child was being out of order. Parental love disciplines and corrects, but never abuses.

Easily frustrated: This means that because an inner turmoil occurs that could cause an inner wound, it is easy to become easily frustrated with everyday chores and responsibilities.

Escapism: As a result of inner turmoil, it is easy to desire to escape or suppress reality. This can be in the form of overeating, drinking, smoking, porn, spending binges, etc. When a person indulges in escapism, addictions can form, and open the door to spirits of addiction. This makes the addictions virtually impossible to break.

STOP AND JOURNAL your thoughts by writing down which of the above emotions you are currently feeling and use this scripture to develop a prayer of mediation: **LUKE 9:23-24 (NLT)** *23 Then he said to the crowd, "If any of you wants to be my follower, you must give up your own way, take up your cross daily, and follow me. 24 If you try to hang on to your life, you will lose it. But if you give up your life for my sake, you will save it."*

_____

_____

_____

_____

_____

_____

_____.

Retaliation urges: because of built-up hate and anger as a result of unforgiveness, somebody who has a festering inner wound will find it easy to retaliate or snap back at those who offend them or step on their toes.

Irresponsible behavior: inner pain has a way of consuming a person's mind, and eventually this can take on a careless approach to life. It is hard to feel good about yourself if you have an inner wound, and if you don't feel good about yourself, it will begin to show in your lifestyle.

STOP AND JOURNAL your thoughts by writing down which of the above emotions you are currently feeling and use this scripture to develop a prayer of mediation: **PSALM 42:9-11 (NLT)** *9 "O God my rock," I cry, "Why have you forgotten me? Why must I wander around in grief, oppressed by my enemies?" 10 Their taunts break my bones. They scoff, "Where is this God of yours?" 11 Why am I discouraged? Why is my heart so sad? I will put my hope in God! I will praise him again—my Savior and my God!"*

_____

_____

_____

_____

_____

_____

_____

_____.

Irrational expectations of others: Somebody who has been wounded may set high expectations for those around them. They feel that others ought to hold up to unrealistic standards and are very intolerable to any mistakes made. They find it hard to forbear (put up with) one another as the Bible commands of us (Colossians 3:13).

STOP AND JOURNAL your thoughts by writing down which of the above emotions you currently feeling and use this scripture to develop a prayer of mediation: **COLOSSIANS 3:13 (NLT)** 13 *Make allowance for each other's faults, and forgive anyone who offends you. Remember, the Lord forgave you, so you must forgive others.*

_____

_____

_____

_____

_____

_____

_____.

Perfectionism: A person who has an emotional wound may also be performance driven. Perhaps they felt like no matter what they did, they could never please a parent or authority figure, and later on in life, that rejection wound causes the person to be a performer. This happens to the point where the individual are never satisfied and burned out by their efforts.

STOP AND JOURNAL your thoughts by writing down which of the above emotions you are currently feeling and use this scripture to develop a prayer of mediation: **GALATIANS 1:10 (NLT)** *Obviously, I'm not trying to win the approval of people, but of God. If pleasing people were my goal, I would not be Christ's servant.*

_____

_____

_____

_____

_____

_____.

Feelings of hopelessness: I believe this is also a common result of unresolved inner wounds. Since the love of God is blocked in your life, it becomes hard to see why He would love or care for you, and therefore you become an easy target for feelings of hopelessness.

Overreaching Drive: When you suffer from an emotional wound, it can create a sense of void in your life's meaning, thus driving you to find meaning and purpose and happiness in various ways some healthy and some unhealthy. This could be in the form of college degrees, careers, financial success, etc. Instead of appreciating the person who God has made (YOU!), you find yourself chasing what you think will bring true happiness and purpose to your life.

Obsessive Compulsive Disorder or OCD: It is my belief that Obsessive Compulsive Disorder (OCD) often involves emotional wounds that were never fully healed. This is especially true with people who have bondages to self-hate, self-resentment, self-unforgiveness, etc.

Hostility towards God, self, and others: Because of bound up emotions, a person can tend to feel hostile towards God, other people in their life, or even themselves. This is usually rooted in a form of bitterness against God for not preventing something from happening to you, bitterness against somebody who has wronged or harmed you emotionally, or bitterness against yourself for failures that you've fallen into yourself.

> **STOP AND JOURNAL** your thoughts by writing down which of the above emotions you are currently feeling and use this scripture to develop a prayer of mediation: **GALATIANS 5:1 (NLT)** *So Christ has truly set us free. Now make sure that you stay free, and don't get tied up again in slavery to the law.*

_____

_____

_____

_____

_____

_____.

BE HONEST WITH YOURSELF!

Are you having physical and emotional symptoms? One way of knowing that we need healing is that our body won't let us "be normal" or carry on with our usual day-to-day activities. You might be having trouble sleeping, eating, or concentrating. You might be crying, "numb," or feeling panic. These physical signs can be scary, but think of these symptoms as trying to get you to pay more attention to something. If your normal functioning is disrupted, pay attention!! This next exercise will help you see what signs and symptoms are calling for your attention.

EXERCISE: Getting in touch with your feelings

Circle what you are feeling and experiencing RIGHT NOW:

Not get being able to sleep Can't wake up in the morning Waking up in the middle of the night. Not wanting to get up Having nightmares	Unable to eat Don't have any appetite Eating too much Crying a lot Feeling "heavy hearted"	Agitated Anxious Not wanting to be alone. Being nervous and not able to sit still
Sad/depressed Numb or not interested in normal activities Distracted Hurting one's self Drinking too much alcohol or using drugs to cope	Irritable or angry with others, particularly spouse. Crying or upset when seeing children or babies Not wanting to see people Don't feel "safe" with most people	Unable to respond to one's children Fearful Not wanting to leave one's house Short attention span at work/school

Think of the above feelings you have circled. They are physical and emotional inner complaints that have been "knocking on your door," and get your attention quite often. The more you try to ignore them, the harder they try to get your attention. For example, it can be very alarming to feel depressed or not to be able to function in your regular activities. It can be very bad to experience non-fruitful relationships due to a bad breakup from a previous relationship. But if those feelings or symptoms get you to pay attention and start healing then they have served a good purpose. When you start acknowledging your feelings, these symptoms should improve, sometimes quite quickly.

Those circled above are what I call emotional wounds and are making you vulnerable! Things that other women usually don't pay attention to may prevent YOU from sleeping just because YOU have some wounds that haven't healed. The more wounds you have the more you'll find that small things bother you and you will eventually become over-sensitive to every critical comment even if the other person didn't really mean to offend you. The more wounds you have the less joy you will feel; because, every now and then something will touch your wound(s) and make you feel bad. You may think you can heal your wounds by forgetting about them or by being alone and "busy" as I once did, however, this strategy always works against you. Living, laughing, and loving can't be really achieved unless you get rid of your emotional wounds, or at least start dealing with them. Heal your wounds. Face your problems. Stop turning your back to them, and you will kill depression. The Apostle Paul says, "The temptations in your life are no different from what others experience. And God is faithful. He will not allow the temptation to be more than you can stand. When you are tempted, he will show you a way out so that you can endure (1 Corinthians 10:13).

Here's an example: I can recall a "We-time" lunch with a mentee, a time where we came together to have lunch, brunch or do some type of activity together. In most cases, these "We-time" moments are a time where we catch up and discuss life-challenges or praise reports. *Sidebar:* As a spiritual mentor to women I have a belief for myself and my mentees: we do life together. I believe it is important to carve out some time to build healthy communication and understanding to what your mentee is experiencing. In my book, *"My Life Matters,"* I discuss the importance of creating a mentor relationship that effectively ministers to the heart of your mentee and causes their authentic transformation. Hence, she mentioned she was sad and could not understand why. Therefore, I begin to probe more and asked her to remember what was going on for her to feel this way. This is a strategy I use to help women filter through their thoughts and utilize their discernment. In other words, they are encouraged to think back to what they were discussing, thinking, or listening to prior to having this feeling of emotion. She began to discuss the events of the day, and I could see her countenance change or her face light up. I call these moments "AHA!!". Meaning, she was awakened by a heavenly action. She remembered exactly what happened. It happened at the time of her completing an assignment in preparation for our "We-time" lunch. She remembers answering questions of what's working and what's not working.

Understand my dear, it is my mentee's desire to experience love again. It is her desire to be an entrepreneur. At the time, she wrote down her expectations, she felt inadequate. She did not see anything positive. She felt she should have been further along than she was. This is the trick of the enemy. We look at our circumstance from a distorted viewpoint, but God wants you to look again (1 Kings 18:43). This very word liberated my mentee and her mind was renewed (Romans 12:1-2). Guess what, God wants to do the same for you. He wants you to be free and free indeed (John 8:36).

How do you normally cope with life's situations? Do you usually try to "work it out by yourself," or just try to forget about it? So, we need to take those very feelings we have identified and really see our strength as a result. Before you can heal any of these wounds you should first identify their location, or in other words, know the reason behind that wound. Don't be passive but seek your answers and trace your wounds to their origin. If critical comments bother you then don't just stay like that. Search the web, read more, think, and analyze the issue until you know the root cause and when you finally know the cause healing the wound itself will become much simpler.

Since you are opened to the possibility of change, you can discover the root cause of all your emotional wounds. Remember, if you tried to escape or forget about these wounds they aren't going to leave you alone, but they will remind you of their existence with each rejection, critical comment or whenever you get dumped or ignored. Don't leave your wounds like that; Heal them. This process in your journey is important, and I challenge you to don't skip over this part of your healing. I know you don't want to go there and experience the pain. But sometimes experiencing pain helps you to understand the purpose behind the pain. I know it does not make sense at this very moment but trust me, well not me, trust God. He is right here alongside you, to urge you through the power of the Holy Spirit to run on, run on. Don't stop. I often say, yieldedness to the Lord's will is key to being able to accept changes gracefully.

THERE IS PURPOSE IN YOUR PAIN, IT'S JUST ACCEPTING IT

My dear, I have come to discover there comes a season where we feel our lives are incomplete. We want something's very much, and we don't seem to be content without them. Sometimes this lack of contentment is what the bible calls covetousness. This means wanting other than what God has ordained for us. We miss the mark of discerning this season God has us in by not realizing He is trying to give us his desire for something in His will. We must understand that even though we have a desire, it may not necessarily be the time; because, we are not ready yet. As a result of our desired timing and God's timing not being in alignment, frustration comes, and spiritual temper tantrums begin. This is also the place in life where you become tormented by the fact that you cannot have it. What happens next is that the flesh gets in the way, so you develop "anorexia of the soul" which is a state of emotional and spiritual exhaustion.

In this empty condition you feel cast-off, drained and used up. You have little energy to deal with people. Everyone gets on your nerves. As a result, you seek ways to escape and detach from it all. You pretend you are being fruitful. You pretend all is well. You pretend life is good. But, this pretention is like driving a car that is misaligned and veers to the right. It takes constant effort to stay on course. As soon as you relax and loosen grip, you end up swerving again. You can't keep faking it, until you make it because sooner or later, the other "you" will come out and take over. Keeping your life and all of the other "roles" you have going in the right direction can be difficult when your inner life is out of line. Instead of pretending that everything is straight while struggling with steering, why not just go to the master mechanic "God" for a soul alignment. Today is your day. This is your hour. Enough is enough. God is saying there's power in your pain.

That is exactly where Hannah is in 1 Samuel Chapter 1. She was a woman who very much wanted to have children, but she was unable to conceive. She was barren. Hannah's identity was tied up with having children. To make matters even worse, she was in a three-way relationship between herself, Elkanah, and Peninnah. For the bible says that Peninnah would take every chance she got to throw up in Hannah's face that she could give Elkanah children and Hannah could not. Imagine if Hannah was with us today. I would like to think this is how her life would be: every time Hannah would sign in to her FaceBook page she would see pictures and post of Peninnah talking about her children and her relationship with Elkanah in her timelines. Then, she finally changes her security settings where people have to get approvals to post tags onto her page, but it still doesn't change the fact that Peninnah is able to post things on her page. The Bible says, year after year, Hannah experienced the same pain. Year after year, she endured the same tormenting from Peninnah. Year after year, her feeling of lack of purpose increased.

Elkanah was aware of the drama. He was aware of Hannah's pain, and he tried to compensate her by giving her a double portion blessing as evidence of his love for her. He did this all despite the social criticism and his rights under civil law to divorce Hannah. We could imagine if Hannah was here right now and had a microphone, she would probably testify out of frustration: "How can opening a bank account in my name and depositing lump sums of money yearly, Mercedes Benz Cl65, buying me Christian Louboutin shoes, expensive gifts, ever going to compensate me for my pain?" I have Peninnah over here that viciously delights in provoking me and reminding me of my inadequacy through social media, First Lady brunches, and in the sanctuary.

Peninnah represents people who accept social paradigms without examining them. These individuals often act out in jealously and envy. In other words, these are women who are prideful and provocative in criticizing others. They always have something negative to say and try very hard to tear others down. Essentially and sadly, these women never have anything positive to say. It's like the more Elkanah focused on Hannah, the more jealous and envious Peninnah became. According to the Bible, for Hannah it was year after year, same pain. Year after year the same pain – does this sound familiar? Year after year, the same depression. Year after year the same prayer poured out with like childlike hope only to discover years of disappointment have intervened until there seemed to be no prayers left to pray. We are all like Hannah at times - tired of waiting for a birth to happen.

Is this you my dear? Like Hannah, are you also tired; because, year after year you experience the same unemployment. Year after year, you experience the same health issues. Year after year, you experience the same financial problems. Year after year, you experience the same problem on your job exists. Year after year, you live through the same issues in your marriage, the same issues with your children. Year after year, you are the bridesmaid and not the bride. Well I'm here to tell you that Hannah has a solution for you. Hannah finds out the key to keeping your sanity is that you don't respond to people, but you take it to God. What's awesome about this narrative of Hannah is that she never responds to Peninnah. She never responds to her vocal darts that are shot at her. She ignores her. After-all Hannah is looking for a blessing. Hannah says why waste my time and energy on someone whose taunting me; because, I don't have the blessing yet. I need to focus my time and energy on the one who can fix anything I need and that someone is the Lord. The question I have posed when reading this passage is this: "Why did Peninnah always take the opportunity to provoke her and make Hannah unhappy while they were in the temple?" It is important to understand that you can't allow people to distract you from your purpose in God. Although, you have not received what you prayed for yet, just know that God is still in control and the promise will come to pass.

Hannah's world was both beautifully flawed and flaky. Her heart was bruised and bleeding from the constant attacks of a jealous woman. The scars and scratches on her psyche are almost visible as you look into this passage in verse 8. It reveals to us that Hannah's discontentment with her situation was complicated. It was so complicated, so much so that her own husband did not recognize her distress: *Her husband Elkanah said, "Oh, Hannah, why are you crying? Why aren't you eating? And why are you so upset? Am I not of more worth to you than ten sons?"* Don't deal with people who cannot discern your distress.

See it was obvious that she was barren, and he understood that. Elkanah knew her body, but he did not know her needs. He gave her things, but he did not know her wants. He knew her name but did not know her heart. He was able to touch her body but was out of touch with her mind. Imagine Hannah saying, "how can you sleep with me and not know me? This thing is not about you!"

Elkanah was getting it (wink). But, he did not get it. He did not realize she was struggling with more than her ability to give birth. It was more than that. It was her deep desire to have God's approval. In those days, a barren woman in that culture felt dishonored by God. She thought He was denying her a part in fulfilling His promise. Human relationships are important, but our critical need is to know that we have the approval of God. He alone can satisfy our deepest needs. There is a principle in the Bible to encourage us without faith *it is* impossible to please *Him,* for he who comes to God must believe that He is, and *that* He is a rewarder of those who diligently seek Him. (Hebrews 11:6, NKJV). God will give you the courage to rise out of your situation.

The Bible further states, Hannah ate, pulled herself together, slipped away quietly, and entered the sanctuary. Verse nine in the King James Version says, Hannah arose after they had finished eating and drinking in Shiloh. See on this particular trip to Shiloh, Hannah barely makes it through the meal. Somehow, she fortifies herself against Peninnah's cruel remarks and actions. She finds her way into the temple. *The word arose in the Hebrew is qūwm (koom) whose root meaning is to rise or get up.* She was depressed, but Hannah rose.

She was barren, but Hannah rose. She was worn out mentally, but Hannah rose. In other words, if you could just get up, you are doing one of the best things you can do as God works out your situation. To get up is a sign that what you are going through is not about to get the best of you. To get up is making a statement to the devil, that he has had his last day of messing with your mind. Today, right now this very moment in your life, is the day to make a statement to yourself no more Kleenex. No more woe is me sermons. No more calling my prayer partners to get their opinion about my situation. Promise yourself that "no matter how long I've been down, I'm about to get up."

Hannah decided that her life was going to change. I call this "Decisive Faith." Faith that says, why should I sit here another year and cry about this situation. Why should I sit here another year and allow this thing to hold me captive? What is the thing holding you captive? As the daughter of the King, you clearly have rights. Therefore, what does it profit, my friend, if you say you have faith but do not have works? Faith by itself, if it does not have works, is dead (James 2:14,17, NKJV) James is saying true faith transforms our conduct as well as our thoughts. If our lives remain unchanged, we don't truly believe the truths we claim to believe.

Question, are you discontent because you want something that God has not planned for you or that you are not ready for? The Bible says, in verse 10 rushed in soul, Hannah prayed to God and cried and cried—inconsolably. Then she made a vow:

Oh, God-of-the-Angel-Armies, If you'll take a good, hard look at my pain, If you'll quit neglecting me and go into action for me By giving me a son, I'll give him completely, unreservedly to you. I'll set him apart for a life of holy discipline.Hannah lets us know here that if you really looking for change, then we have to deal with some internal turmoil. We should deal with these desires by pouring out our heart to God. See pouring out your heart to the Lord is always safe, and it is always wise. Why? Prayer does not make God see things as we see them; it helps us see things as God sees them. Hannah realized it was something more she had to do. She knew she had to go deeper in her relationship. Therefore, Hannah made a vow to the Lord. Whatever was causing her discontentment, she was going to offer it back to the Lord. Making a vow or an oath to the Lord is no small thing. When God does say yes to our requests, He does so in order for us to be better servants for Him. This means we should be ready to offer back to Him the gift He has given to us. It is good to ask God to take care of the problem that is making us discontent, but to do so understanding that He may have a different plan in mind.

Therefore, if you are praying for a car, would you be willing to pick up individuals and bring them to church? If you are praying for a house, would you be willing to help individuals who are need of a place to stay temporarily. If you are praying for a job, would you let your light shine and witness for Him? If you are praying for a financial breakthrough, would you be willing to increase your giving in the Kingdom. God gives us blessings to glorify Him, not to satisfy our selfish desires (Ecclesiastes 6:2, NIV). In the midst of her prayer, the Priest Eli saw her and tried to judge her condition based upon what he perceived about the way she was acting without knowing what was wrong with her. It so happened that as she continued in prayer before God, Eli was watching her closely. Hannah was praying in her heart, silently. Her lips moved, but no sound was heard. Eli jumped to the conclusion that she was drunk. He approached her and said, "You're drunk! How long do you plan to keep this up? Sober up, woman!" Don't allow the distractions of people's opinion to get in the way.

I have discovered first hand that Satan loves to distract us with criticism, and he tries to get us to use it on others as well as ourselves. We judge prematurely and try to correct others before we know what they're saying. That's what Eli the priest did when Hannah was crying out to God. He interrupted her prayer and accused her of being drunk. Eli was so carnal minded that he immediately assumed the worst. Let me help you understand Eli's mindset in verse 14. The world had lost the way to God. And Eli was seeing the debris of what had been torn down during the chaotic days of the Judge

(Judges 21:25). Therefore, he had little understanding and little compassion. In those days, drunk people and bad women were not an unusual sight in the house of God. As a matter of fact, the Bible tells us Eli's own sons slept with the women who gathered at the door of the tabernacle. Therefore, Eli didn't think it was anything spiritual. Hence, it was something he wasn't used to seeing and had never experienced. It was simply outside of the parameters of his experience, and he defined it as Hannah being drunk.

There are times in our lives where our response shows our level of maturity in life's challenging situations. Hannah's reveals her level of maturity by responding positively. You would think now she would lose it and go off; but Hannah's response: *"Oh no, sir—please! I'm a woman hard used. I haven't been drinking. Not a drop of wine or beer. The only thing I've been pouring out is my heart, pouring it out to God. Don't for a minute think I'm a bad woman. It's because I'm so desperately unhappy and in such pain that I've stayed here so long (verses 15-16)."* Hannah explained that she was not drunk but poured out soul before the Lord. Eli did not discern what was going on with Hannah. There is another hard lesson learned here: Often the people we expect to understand; don't understand. We see in these passages of scripture, it was not until Eli found out that she was seeking the Lord. Eli answered her, *"Go in peace. And may the God of Israel give you what you have asked of him (verse 17)."*

Again, Hannah responds maturely *"Think well of me—and pray for me!" she said, and went her way. Then she ate heartily, her face radiant (Verse 18)."* What amazing faith Hannah had! This reminds me of the kind of faith prayer that Jesus told us to pray in Mark 11:23-24: *"Have faith in God," Jesus answered. "I tell you the truth, if anyone says to this mountain, 'Go, throw yourself into the sea,' and does not doubt in his heart but believes that what he says will happen, it will be done for him. Therefore, I tell you, whatever you ask for in prayer, believe that you have received it, and it will be yours."* It may help to remember how you have coped with stressful experiences in the past, such as the death of a loved one, a divorce in the family, or other loss. David said to himself, "Why am I discouraged? Why is my heart so sad? I will put my hope in

God! I will praise him again— my Savior and my God! (Psalm 42:5-6)." There are times in our lives where we can only focus on the negativity of our situation. However, this passage above gives us hope. There is light. At this time, I would like for you to take a moment and recall what God has already done for you in the past. Trust and believe this is where your strength will come in.

Exercise: Calling on my strength

List some of these experiences:

What did God help you get through, an/or what character attributes or what resources outside of yourself helped you get through helped you get through? _____

_____
_____
_____.

Make a list in your journal (or below) of those strengths that got you through and other strengths you have: _____

_____
_____
_____.

Make a list of what you learned from these experiences: _____

_____
_____
_____
_____.

You have started some hard work. You have declared your intentions to heal and began to identify clearly what healing will look like for you. You have remembered strengths that have helped you before. Take a few moments to let all this sit with you. Then take three deep, slow breaths and begin to think about what is now calling your attention in your daily life. You will return later and move forward. Remember, this is a process and change take time. All of the steps in this resource will help you with the process of accepting your current reality. Meaning, where you are in the process and taking ownership and acceptance of your part.

STRATEGY FOUR
ACCEPT YOUR CURRENT REALITY

The reality is _____. Each of us can complete the rest of this statement. Whether we didn't get a job we really wanted, our relationship didn't work out, a close friend is doing something we don't approve of, or we got stopped for a speeding ticket, each of us must deal with events and situations that are not ideal at some point. Sometimes facing reality isn't the easiest thing to do but accepting our current situation can make us joyful in the present and lead to a better future. Accepting our situation doesn't mean we have to like it or that we support the conditions that lead us there. Refusing to accept our reality, though, can have major consequences on our mental and physical health, leading to anxiety, chronic physical pain, or bodily harm caused by distracting behaviors like eating unhealthy foods, drinking too much alcohol, using drugs, or having unprotected sex with multiple men.

Earlier in my walk as a believer, I had this false belief that God was punishing me for past sins that I committed. It was not until I matured in the Lord and realized I was not being punished, but the consequences I endured were a result of the poor decisions I made to sabotage my spiritual growth. There is a difference between punishment and consequence. Punishments are used to impose suffering of some kind and to make it clear who is in control. They are often unrelated to the problem behavior. For example, as a teenager my mom would take away my telephone privileges because of my behavior. The behavior, however, was being mean to my brother or a call coming from school related to my conduct. Honestly, these behaviors were most often given in moments of anger and frustration. The result of most punishments is that it instills fear and resentment. Punishment made me feel reluctant to admit my mistakes, and most importantly, it had little, if any, effect on my future behavior. Why? Because there were no consequences because of my behavior.

As I grew older, I learned consequences, on the other hand, are designed to teach me to learn from my mistakes. They encourage good behavior and taught me to engage in more proactive problem solving. Ideally, consequences end up teaching me that I am in control of, and responsible for, my behavior. As a result, the root cause was my choice to become disobedient.

🌩 WISDOM KEY APPLICATION

Disobedience brings a wide variety of horrible consequences such as **spiritual, physical, emotional, and mental consequences**.

• **Spiritual consequences:** This term relates to separation from God and union with Satan. It's the worst form of consequence that can ever fall upon us since it determines where we will spend our eternity.

• **Physical consequences:** This term relates to bad things that can happen to us physically or our lives that can be ended so tragically.

• **Emotional consequences:** This term relate to sadness and hurts disobedience can bring to our lives. Disobedience can ruin the very person God wants us to be. Moreover, disobedience can inflict so much emotional pains on us to the extent that we become a slave to bitterness, anger, unforgiveness, and so forth.

• **Mental consequences:** This has to do with the fact that sin burdens the conscience of women. It corrupts and cripples' women's judgment. Sin has a strong hold on memory and negatively the free will. Consequently, there's no genuine peace for those who are living in sin no matter what they/we may say.

We can't play with our personal growth and development. Moreover, we cannot allow the enemy to keep deceiving us. God cannot be mocked. We will reap what we sow (Galatians 6:7). Life is a matter of reaping what you sown. So oftentimes we reap far more than what we've sowed. Despite everything that sin has to offer, the deceptive pleasures that we may experience are not worth the price that we must pay eventually. Sin is very controlling, powerful, and deceptive by nature. It can become so rooted in our lives; now our lives consist of complexities that have manifested.

WHAT IS COMPLEXITY?

My rule in life is when you know better you do better. Also, God's word says we parish due to lack of knowledge (Hosea 4:6). Therefore, I am always researching and learning new things. Knowledge is power, once imparted on the inside of me I can gain wealth (Deuteronomy 8:18). Hence, complexity was a new word for me. In my research, I learned the definition as found in American Counseling Association "it is a core pattern of emotions, memories, perceptions, and wishes in the personal unconscious organized around a common theme." Powerful right? Each of us may have many thoughts, emotions, memories, feelings of inferiority, triumphs, bitterness, and determinations centering on that one aspect of our life.

To fully accept some situations, it is important to acknowledge the role you played in causing the problem. Ask yourself questions related to your situation to help you work towards solutions. For example, I can use myself. For the past several years, my health and wellness has been inconsistent. So, I would ask myself after every do-over: self, if you are overweight and wish you weighed less, think about the reasons you are overweight. Do you eat a healthy diet of natural vegetables, fruits, and grains? Do you exercise regularly? Is there someone holding you accountable? The answer is always no, no, and no!

Or I could ask you: if you are unhappy with a relationship, consider why you continue to stay with this person. Are you afraid that you might end up alone? Do you worry that separating or divorcing will lead to financial problems? Or, if you hate your job, ask yourself why you continue to work there. Do you need more education or training to do what you really want to do? And if so, why haven't you gotten it yet? Are there other jobs you could be applying for? Are you staying because it is comfortable, even if unhealthy for your well-being? Can you see the complexities in these statement questions?

🗯 WISDOM KEY APPLICATION

Through the Word of God, you will get the wisdom you need to handle the complex issues of life:

PHILIPPIANS 4:8 *Finally, brothers, whatever is true, whatever is honorable, whatever is just, whatever is pure, whatever is lovely, whatever is commendable, if there is any excellence, if there is anything worthy of praise, think about these things.*

JAMES 3:13–18 *13 Who is wise and understanding among you? By his good conduct let him show his works in the meekness of wisdom. 14 But if you have bitter jealousy and selfish ambition in your hearts, do not boast and be false to the truth. 15 This is not the wisdom that comes down from above, but is earthly, unspiritual, and demonic. 16 For where jealousy and selfish ambition exist, there will be disorder and every vile practice.17 But the wisdom from above is first pure, then peaceable, gentle, open to reason, full of mercy and good fruits, impartial and sincere.18 And a harvest of righteousness is sown in peace by those who make peace.*

In reflecting on these previous scriptures, the questions I would ask are: what are the parts of your *complex* experience? Every issue we experience is different. The choices on how we deal with our life situations, our past, our future hopes, and dreams - all that and more - are complex and up to us. Therefore, in this next exercise, you will revisit how you came to make the choices you made up to this point in your life.

EXERCISE: My Own Experience

Think back to how you made the choices you made until now. In your journal, write the story of your life choices with your *non-dominant hand (the opposite hand your write with)* and include the people who were part of the decision and whether they were helpful or not. Include all the things you thought about. This exercise is longer and may take 30 minutes or more of your concentrated time. Do you have time to focus on this right now? As a suggestion my dear, read over the exercise and then come back and do the work a little later. Put yourself on your to-do-list for some "Me-time" that way you can really give attention to this exercise. Giving yourself the time, you need helps the healing process. Now, think about the individuals, life circumstances, and dreams that were factors in your decision.

First, to help you get started, I have listed some personal factors myself and other women (at their requests no names mentioned) have considered in their decisions. Read over these factors and **circle** any of the sample factors below that were part of your decision-making. You may also add some factors that are not listed here. Again, I want you to use your own words but utilizing your non-dominant hand.

Sense of Self	Stability
Husband	Job
Boyfriend	Education
Children	Religion/Spirituality
Family	Co-worker
Best friend	Others I can list (you may have your own)

Sometimes an experience can make you question who you are, and your feelings about yourself. Do you have other concerns or self-doubts? Write them in your journal with your non-dominant hand (the opposite hand you write with). It's good to get these thoughts out of our heads and on paper so we can really look at them see how real they are. This last part of the exercise reminds you of the **complex** nature of your decision. Choose up to **three factors** that were important in you making the choice you did. They may be like the examples as some women journaled about their relationships factors with husband or boyfriend.

Now, what are the most important factors for you?

For example, I had a problem with sense of self. Therefore, I journaled the following factors about my sense of self.

Sense of Self: "I don't feel like myself because..." As a result, "I don't know who I am anymore because...Therefore, drugs and alcohol were a way for me to cope with my situation about myself."

Husband: "I got married; because, I was in love." "I felt that marrying him was the right thing to do." "I did not want to get a divorce, but I had no choice." "I was embarrassed; because, we had a big wedding, and we put too much money in it already."

Boyfriend: "I am with him because I don't want to be alone." "There is something about him and I can't put my finger on it, but I need to be with him." "All my other girlfriends are married, and I am getting too old. The clock is tick, tick, tocking!"

Now breathe for a minute. Now, you take three factors of your own and write in your journal (non-dominant hand). Re-read your story and as you look at all the factors that you considered in your choice, you can see why it is important to look at all the separate parts to be able to move forward in a healthy way. I know this is hard work, but you will be so emotionally healed.

Here's what has happened, this story has been recorded and replayed in your mind for years. It has become your being and keeps you from becoming. Your life is stagnant; because, of this very story. This woman is on the inside of you is screaming "LET ME OUT, SO I CAN BE CREATIVE AND HEAL!" If you noticed I had you to write in a technique to let you see where your mind is being blocked and what you see in your situation that needs healing. Your non-dominant hand shows awkwardness, neglection, weakness and somewhat childlike behaviors. This speaks volume because it helps us to realize God says it is time to mature in these factors that has caused areas of our lives to be stuck. If you think about it, our dominant hand has been trained, practiced, and developed manual skill, strength, and self-control. Meaning, God wants us to develop a voice, use discernment and make the right choices in life. It is not what others say about us that matters, but it is about what we say about ourselves that matters.

Understand this, when strong emotions come up in your everyday life, let your non-dominant hand draw or write them out. If you are visual like me, you tend to express your emotions in color. For example, when I am angry; I say phrases like "I was so angry I could see red". At the end, I tend to write in my journal the day's event, I include all situations good or bad. I filter through what brought me to this space of anger, and then write in blue how I could have managed my emotion better. Color pencils work very well, or you can get colored gel pens. I challenge you to try this technique out. It helps with managing your emotions as well as hold yourself accountable in what you say because the tongue has the power of life and death, and those who love it will eat its fruit (Proverbs 18:21). Next time, I would T.H.I.N.K by filtering through the emotion I am feeling at the time:

💭 WISDOM KEY APPLICATION

T – is it True?
H – is it Helpful?
I – is it Inspiring?
N – is it Necessary?
K – is it Kind?

If any one of the question is no, then I do not respond. This process will bring more improvement in your own self-talk.

STRATEGY FIVE
IMPROVE YOUR SELF TALK

WRITING NEW MESSAGES FOR YOU, ABOUT YOURSELF
There are a lot of negative messages in our culture about women. So, you may have to work hard to challenge these and create messages that are both true and healing. You will probably need help and support with this process. Replacing negative thoughts with positive ones is a good way to help you feel better. Whenever you have a negative thought, try to replace it with a positive version of that thought. If someone you love passes away, and you constantly think that your life will never be joyful again, and then this can affect your outlook on life. To counteract these thoughts, you might tell yourself something like, "I will experience love and joy again."

Or, if you have lost your job and money is tight, then you might focus on something positive that you are doing to improve your situation, such as, "I am learning effective ways to manage the money that I have." Or you may decree scripture "God has given me power to gain wealth (Deuteronomy 8:18)". Think about some negative words, statements, or *ways of describing you or your decision* in the last exercise. These negative messages do not help you heal or move you closer to 'coming back into your life.' We will gradually find new messages that help healing and leave the negative messages behind.

These next exercises have three parts. It could very easily take you 30 minutes to over an hour to really think about and write down all the messages you might be telling yourself or hearing from others. This is an important step; because, as we know, healing happens from the inside out. You may see a need for a break after the first two parts.

EXERCISE: WHAT AM I HEARING ABOUT MYSELF?

In this 3-part exercise, you will look at all the messages about yourself that you are receiving from your own "head" and what you are hearing from others. Then write some new messages that are more positive and healing.

PART 1: INTERNAL MESSAGES: WHAT ARE YOU TELLING YOURSELF ABOUT YOURSELF?

Let's start with the difficult and often hurtful **negative** messages. What are some of the negative messages inside your head? Review what you wrote about the factors in your decision in Strategy Four. Choose one – or more – of the most important factors. Write them in the space provided after the examples offered on the next page. Then, write 1- 3 sentences about what is troubling you in the space below. If the factors in your decision are not listed in the examples below use your journal to write your sentences. Here are some example messages:

EXAMPLES:

FACTOR #1 UNDER FAMILY: MY MOTHER FORCED ME TO HAVE AN ABORTION.

- I am not trustworthy in my mother's eyes.
- I deserve to be miserable for disappointing my mother.
- I hate her for making me kill my child.

FACTOR #2 UNDER RELATIONSHIP WITH BOYFRIEND: I WAS ALREADY A SINGLE PARENT, STRUGGLING TO CARE FOR MY CHILD.

I went searching on the dating online service; I should have put my daughter first. I am glad that abusive relationship is over. But, I must now deal with a rebellious daughter acting out in school.

NOW, YOU WRITE OUT ONE OF THE ACTUAL FACTORS YOU CIRCLED IN THE LAST SECTION.

Then, write down 1- 3 negative messages you are hearing connected with that factor – just like in the examples above. If you feel like doing more, choose another factor you circled, or as many of the factors as you want. Write 1 – 3 negative messages you 'hear' in your head about those factors.

1. Factor # 1:

Messages I hear in my head: _____

_____

_____.

2. Factor #2:

Messages I hear in my head: _____

_____

_____.

3. Factor #3:

Messages I hear in my head: _____

_____

_____.

Please make a note; you may be hearing some positive messages too. If so, this is super! Write them down here and we will look at them in the next section.

PART 2: EXTERNAL MESSAGES: WHAT ARE YOU HEARING FROM OTHERS?

Now, think about the messages others in your life are sending you. Maybe they say them out loud; **maybe** you 'just know.' Even those close to you may send you negative messages. It may help to identify the people and write the message you are hearing from them here. For example, let's use the "boyfriend factor" they may be saying:

"You should have had wisdom about going on an online dating site. You're irresponsible. You're stupid." "Why didn't you just leave" "If you play, you pay; you should have known better" "Get over it already; that happened to you once before."

NOW YOU WRITE DOWN SOME EXTERNAL MESSAGES YOU MAY HEAR ABOUT YOUR SITUATIONS OR CIRCUMSTANCES.

Now, write what messages other people are sending to you. Include who is saying what. (If you are hearing some positive messages, AWESOME! Write them down and we will look at them in the next section.)

_____

_____

_____

_____.

PART 3: HEALING MESSAGES: WRITING NEW MESSAGES FOR YOURSELF

Sometimes, new words are needed. This is particularly true in coping with an abortion experience. You may not feel able to talk about this experience with others, or it may be misunderstood by some people. To resist the negative messages that we are hearing, we need to create some new positive messages for ourselves that are both true and healing. We're going to create new messages that remind you of your own goodness and help you to accept your own human-ness, even your own "imperfection." In this part of the exercise, you may want to include someone else who can help you remember the good in you and help you think of new messages for your healing.

You will want to consider your own **compassion.** You may want to look at how **forgiving** you are of others. You can offer that same compassion and forgiveness to yourself. It takes **strength** and **courage** to refuse to accept the negative messages our culture often holds for women and their choices. To get you started, I have listed some of the negative messages from the first part of this exercise and offered suggestions to create more positive messages for yourself. Try these. If they apply to you write your own responses under the examples. Remember, as you work through these examples, everyone is different. For some, all of these and more are true. For others, only one or two seem right. And, for many, there are additional messages for which we have not provided an example. These are here just to get you started. Take what you need from these examples and write your own responses based on your experience.

Take the time to think about God's goodness. There is an internal conflict keeping you from emotional freedom. The choices you have made in your life onto this moment have hindered you from progressing. Internal conflict is what I call a disagreement, struggle or battle within one's self over issues or principles. The Apostle Paul said, "I want you to know how much I am struggling for you and those at Laodicea and for all who have not me personally (Colossians 2:1)." Likewise, I want the same for you my dear. Positive messages will help you heal. This exercise may be the hardest - and the most important! *You deserve peace.*

EXAMPLE #1: FORGIVING YOURSELF: THE HARDEST PERSON TO FORGIVE IS YOU. ONE QUESTION TO ASK IS:

"If your best friend was in the same situation as yours, do you think she could be forgiven?"

Why do you think you are not deserving of forgiveness? Write out how a request or intention to forgive yourself might sound: Do you— or your friends—consider you a "perfectionist?" Can you accept that all humans, including yourself – are imperfect and make mistakes? Yet I still dare to hope when I remember this: The faithful love of the Lord never ends! His mercies never cease (Lamentations 3:19-22). Realize the Lord made you for a purpose, and He designed your personality and gave you the gifts and talents to be who you are. Forgiving yourself means you are ready to move forward an experience a life to live, laugh, and love. Acknowledge and praise God for who you are today.

EXAMPLE #2: "HOW CAN I FEEL GOOD ABOUT MY LIFE AGAIN?" "I HAD THE PERFECT LIFE BEFORE AND NOW I CAN'T SEEM TO GET IT BACK."

Every major life decision changes us and challenges us to look at our lives. We often say that life decisions can be "transformative." This means that we have to look at our lives in new ways and decide about life and whether we can be responsible for new life. In many ways you are the same person as before. In some ways you are different. How you see yourself has been greatly shaped predominantly by the messages you received and internalized from others, from your experiences, and from your own self-talk. When you were a child you had no control of those in authority over you, but since you are an adult woman now, that is no longer the case. You are able to choose those with whom you can associate with, and you can certainly control your self-talk. Therefore, you can play an active role of forming your new destiny. With God being the driver this time, you can never go wrong. Your distorted view of who you are is over, done, and finished today!

What ways are you the same? How are you different? How is your 'difference' now a part of you, of your life, as you move forward? What good has come from this experience?

You have done some challenging work in this exercise. Look back at your list of good qualities and read them aloud to yourself. Read aloud any of your positive statements. Now it's time to take some slow deep breaths and re-connect with your everyday life. Take some time before you go on to the next section. You might want to write down these new messages you just wrote for yourself as separate notes to yourself. Re-read these frequently over the next few days or weeks as you continue your healing journey.

> *Choice is a dialogue with the being who may come to life through our body. We can do no more than to bring our awareness to this sacred conversation. Something is learned from every life and every death. Choice gives us freedom, and choice asks us to accept what we have done."* ~ *Melanie Ermachild*

MAKING POSITIVE MESSAGES MY OWN

I pray you have done some thinking about all the messages you wrote – both negative and positive. Sometimes, things come up that we have kept "jammed down" for years. If you are feeling teary, depressed, or not able to sleep for more than a day or two, consider talking to someone. I don't want you to stop; because, you are feeling "some kind of way." Here's where someone from your "tribe" needs to walk alongside you on this journey of the process. You are doing something new and here is where the enemy starts placing thoughts in your mind that are NOT real. Don't forget you learned in the beginning about the ***Complexity of your Life.*** These same complexities are what the enemy will try to come back and enter your life to discourage you and say this is a waste of time. For once, finish something you have started. You are halfway there.

My dear, it is important to understand this process of improving your self-talk. I am reminded of the time I was having "We-time with my grand-daughter Brielle." She and I were watching "The Help." What a moving and powerful film! If only each of us grew up with that mantra so that the lies of self-doubt and unworthiness would stop haunting us. In the movie, the main character, Aibileen (a black maid and nanny) would say the following words to the 4-year-old child that she cared for every day: "You is kind, You is smart, You is important." In the movie, the mother would ignore her child and treat her badly. The little girl just loved Aibileen and told her that she was her real mom. She felt safe and loved in the arms of her caregiver. Major decisions can bring up old wounds, fears, or memories that we need to deal with to move forward. Asking for help is a sign of strength and courage. For many, help is needed to move forward, to heal. If you are ready, let's move forward to getting your new healing messages into your life. In this exercise, you will take a look at the realities of your life in a new way. It will probably not take as long as the last exercise.

EXERCISE: Making new positive messages part of your life

It took me years to figure out what was bothering me. It had nothing to do with my reality, but the reality contributed to the symptom. I had many things that were troubling me. Interestingly, I became this co-dependent drama queen female. I felt that I did more for others and felt I should receive the same. Therefore, the level of expectation would eventually become a disappointment because of my own false beliefs of what should happen or how they should respond back to me. As you begin to figure out what is troubling you, and finding ways to go forward, you will begin to heal. When you start to feel some progress, you will return to the good parts of your life.

Take stock of your life. Go back to the "Who are You" exercises Part 1 and 2. Read over them and see if your perspective of who you are is the same. Now answer these questions:

- Who needs you?
- Who do you care for?
- What is in your life now that feels good for you?
- What feels healing and empowering?
- What moves you forward, even a little?
- If you were back in your life and felt good about yourself, what could you give to others?

Look at what you wrote in previous exercises, especially those messages that are positive, forgiving, healing, and compassionate. In addition, I challenge you to develop boundaries for yourself by completing the **Flush Out Those False Beliefs** (Appendix I) exercise to help you with this process. Choose one or two new messages to yourself that will address what is troubling you and help you "get back in alignment in a positive space." For example, I wrote for myself: *I am a good person and a good mother, and I made the best decision I could for my life. At the appointed time, God will unite me with the right man for marriage. God sees me as a good thing and this man of valor will obtain favor from God.*

Now, write down your new messages with your dominant hand on a separate piece of paper and post it where you will see them easily and frequently. Re-read them often over the next few days or weeks as well as look in the mirror and encourage yourself.

More Examples:

I need and deserve the support of others. God is infinitely compassionate toward the world and that includes me. I respect myself and my own feelings.

Write your new, more positive messages: _____

_____

_____

_____.

   1. Now, take a minute or two to think about how you feel when you hear these messages.

   2. Go back to the "feelings" exercises at the beginning (**Strategy Three)** and review what you wrote there.

Let's look at how your feelings have shifted. For example, you might describe your shift like: "I am not as hard on myself as I was then." "I feel a little lighter." "I still feel, _____ but I can see some ways to deal with it now."

3. Write your own thoughts and feelings that have 'shifted' or changed here: _____

_____

_____.

Instead, let the Spirit renew your thoughts and attitudes. Put on your new nature, created to be like God—truly righteous and holy (Ephesians 4:24). You are doing great. Take a deep breath. Now please meditate on this scripture and pray God's word and affirm your new message. It's hard to really believe new messages about ourselves. Our own upbringing, experiences, how people treat us, and the messages we get on TV and from society may be reinforcing negative messages. Nonetheless we KNOW our own truths and what makes us feel good about our lives and our world. We are moving forward. We got our groove back and ready to live, laugh and yes love. What has to happen? I am so glad you asked. Now, declare what is rightfully yours.

STRATEGY SIX
WALK THE WALK AND TALK THE TALK

Now the question is what must happen for me to do this? Make up in your mind that you are going forward with your life. You are going to live, laugh, and love. It is going to take strength and courage. You cannot be afraid, and do not panic before them. For the Lord your God will personally go ahead of you. He will neither fail you nor abandon you (Deuteronomy 31:6)". Frankly, in this healing work, you are separating all the many parts of your life decisions and exploring the possibility of each factor. In doing that, you have seen that your life is complex. There is no one simple answer. Healing is a process. It doesn't mean forgetting or pretending you're OK. It takes courage to face your life, to accept love and support from others and time to understand these changes. Most of all, it takes *the desire to heal*.

🗯 WISDOM KEY APPLICATION

Other words for this kind of healing are:

- Integrating the experience into your life
- Incorporating, absorbing, taking in the whole experience
- Atonement 'at-one with'
- An act of forgiveness, making amends

- Affirmation

- Support, encouragement, appreciation

- Acknowledging both losses and blessings

- Being able to share your experience with others.

God allowed me to come to the reality of this experience through the deaths of two special women in my life: Irene J. Patterson (my mother) and Danielle Frank-Lemon (a mentee). Both deaths happened two months apart from each other. I learned a lot about myself through both experiences. Each of these women played major roles in my life but served two different purposes. Mom taught me to be true to self. Danielle taught me to enjoy every moment of your lived experience. Both had the same drive and determination about life and each of them was an example for me to strive to be the best me daily. The best me in their eyes was one of not being in the grind mode constantly. Danielle would often say to me "Hey, Minister P, B.O.S.S. Lady". B.O.S.S. (Bold, Overcomer, Standing, Strong). We would laugh about it. But, later I noticed Danielle would say it in convicting manner. Until one day, I said Danielle, why do you say that to me in a way, I am feeling convicted now." She goes on to explain: "you have been my mentor for five years (at that time). I've noticed your life is not a normal day-to-day. It consists of a day of hustling to the church, hustling to meetings, hustle, hustle and more hustle. You are always on your cellphone, being pressured by yourself to save the world. You are constantly going places networking to build relationships, and finally spending the bits you can with your family. Minister P, this is not healthy. You are my mentor, but you must slow down.

A few months later, I was on the cellphone with one another mentee Pernilla. She and I were speaking one evening. This was our "We-time" to catch up. It was her last year in graduate school; therefore, the face-to-face was impossible because of the projects she had. I have a habit on sitting in the car if I am one the phone with someone while driving to finish the conversation before I walk into my home. On this particularly evening, I heard Pernilla say in very poised and proper voice "Elder P, you seemed to be distracted at the moment, do we need to speak another time? I shared with her, no this is fine I am looking for my cellphone. She says that's fine Elder P, just call me back when you find it. We both laughed and she said, "Elder P, you have a lot going on, slow down Elder, slow down."

Last story, while in a meeting one of the administrators, who is a mentee of mine as well, April, said, "Elder P what are you looking for, I said I am looking for my glasses. In her sweet voice, Elder not sure if that is what's on top of your head, but are those your glasses?" At that moment, I had an "Aha" moment. I went online and took a stress test (see Appendix II). The results were overwhelming. I scored **296 range Medium susceptibility to stress-related illness: Learn and practice relaxation and stress management skills and a healthy well life style.** I decided to reshape my life. I empowered the ten leaders under my leadership. Most importantly, I took a journey of finding fulfillment to gaining better work-life balance.

Amazingly, I did not have to change industries to make this shift. I did not understand at the time when the shift happened. Honestly, God forced the shift to happen. My job at the time shared with me that my position was being eliminated. I understand it now; because, God needed me let go of what I was comfortable and move into the next season where He needed me to be. At that time in my life, God was preparing me. You may ask preparing me (and you) for what? He was preparing me to be authentic in whom I am and to build authentic relationships that were transforming. He nurtured the Fruit of the Spirit: love, joy, peace, patience, kindness, goodness, faithfulness, gentleness, and self-control (Galatians 5:22-23).

Today, I can say my life is quite different. I spend mornings in peace and solidarity before as Dr. Dee Marshall would say I "turn my light on." Meaning, before she started her work day, she spent time with God and herself. I embraced that discipline, and it has aided so much in the development of being a focused individual. After years of preparation, I am focused on my health and wellness where I have found new unique ways to grow and expand who

I am as a woman. I have gained a clearer perspective on what is important in my life, so that I could start working to align my life to that which God says in His word. I am sharing with you an exercise I did personally and exactly what you are going to do next. You have to be willing to do the work to live, laugh, and love. You cannot "half do" the work and expect positive results.

I want to share with you a story. Danielle was one of athletics and she invited me to join a boot camp with her in exercising. We would work out together every Monday morning with other co-laborers which we all men. Well, this one-day Danielle says, "Minister P, I want to help you. You must be tougher. Meaning, when you exercise, it is not "girly girly." It is not being cute. But, you must be disciplined, and I want you to keep up with us. Therefore, you and I can meet on Thursday and review the exercises, that way you will be prepared for Monday." I agreed to join her. Of course, I did not like it. It felt like it was not for me, all the running and sweating. One day, I was not up to it. Therefore, I ignored Danielle's call. I mean this woman called me several times. Then, finally I answered. She says, "Minister P, where are you?" I shared, I am getting ready to go and work out (not true, but I thought it was the right thing to say, so I could get her off the phone). The next words out of her mouth I was not expecting, she said "look out of your window." Danielle drove to my home to pick me up to go and work out. And of course, I submitted.

Fast forward to three weeks later, she and I went to our favorite restaurant for our "cheat day;" For us it was agreed that this day would be on Sundays. I must premise this: Danielle had been praising me all week on my weight lost. She could see the results. As we sat there, eating bread while waiting for our entrees. I began to become faint, sweating, and lose my breathe. I had an "aha" moment. I remembered I had on a full body Spanx and the yeast in the breast was causing my stomach to expand and the Spanx became tighter and tighter. I had to confess to Danielle; which I did not want to do.

The conversation goes as follows: "Danielle, I have a confession.

I have on a Spanx and it is extremely tight and I need to take it off right now; because, I am about to pass out. At that moment, she yelled: Minister P, you have on a SPANX??? At that moment, it seemed as if SPANX was an echo: SPANX SPANX SPANX. I shared: Danielle, this is not the time for your speech. Either you will walk me to ladies' restroom, so I can take off this Spanx or you will have to call 911 because I am about to pass out. So, you know what happened next, we walked to the ladies' restroom and I hear what not to do when Danielle is your fitness coach. Although, this story is humorous, but I wanted to share something so personal to get you to see that God wants us whole in all areas of our lives. I cannot express how the work is so important and you being consistent in completing what you started. There are no shortcuts.

The exercise below is a process you have to be intentional in completing. The more certainty you are as a person, the clearer you will become. To get the most of this exercise, primarily you must put your best effort. Think back to your "Who Am I" exercise, you listed in your pie chart. Now, think about why these were so important to you. Some reason may come to play in your mind easily, while others may be complicated. Your challenge is to get to the root of who you are and what's important and this should activate your faith. Remember the possibilities are endless!

EXERCISE: WHAT HAVE YOU LOST AND WHAT HAVE YOU GAINED?

One way to "bring all the parts back together" is to take stock of what this experience has meant to you. What have you lost and what have you gained? We offer some common examples to get you started. Choose as many of these that apply to your situation, add or write your own.

Here are examples: Write what you feel you have lost:

- "I lost my relationship and my trust in my spouse."

- "I thought I was in charge of my life. Now I don't feel the world is safe or predictable."

- "I lost my mother to breast cancer, what am I going to do? She was my confidant!"

- Here are examples: Write what you feel you have found or gained:

- "I think I appreciate life more—the good and bad, the ups and downs."

- "I see strength in me I did not know I had."

- "I count the blessings of my children and family."

Exercise: Finding your wisdom

As you look at the examples above, think about how you can both acknowledge your loss, and support your decision. In other words, how will you take what you have learned from this experience and make it part of your life? What wisdom have you gained? Phrase it *positively!*

Here are examples to help you get started. Write as many phrases and sentences as seem right.

Some good will come from this experience if I can _____

_____

_____

_____.

I know I made the right choice, so I can pay attention to _____

_____

_____

_____.

I will honor this loss by _____

_____

_____

_____.

The Apostle Paul encourages us "And we know that God causes everything to work together for the good of those who love God and are called according to his purpose for them (Romans 8:28, NLT)". Now write your own words in your journal what this scripture means to you and how it will help your own personal wisdom in making decisions in the future.

This has been quite an effort and you have made a good beginning toward healing. You have done some hard work. Good for you! As you re-enter your life today, focus on all that you 'found' in this experience. I found that setting goals and marking my progress helps in maintaining a healthier lifestyle. Likewise, now that you have done some challenging work, you may have begun to see a difference and to feel things have changed a bit. You may find yourself taking more of an active role in your life. You may notice you are paying more attention to yourself and to those around you, taking more of an interest in life, and enjoying yourself again. I want you to follow the process it took me to heal, become whole, and now I help others. This is an ongoing process so continue to:

🐾 WISDOM KEY APPLICATION

- Pay attention to your feelings.
- Write letters to mark your progress.
- Meditate and pray
- Focus on the positive vibes only
- Support yourself through kind affirmation words

It is common now for many of us to choose a "word-of-the-day" that offers us inspiration or encouragement and reminds us of God's goodness and grace. For the next 21 days, I want you to affirm yourself using each of these words below. Please cut out the words from a magazine, color or decorate them on construction paper, and keep that word with you so you can view it often. Or, make your own. Place your word on your mirror or refrigerator so that you will see it throughout the day.

Grace, Wisdom, Compassion,
Forgiveness, Strength, Courage,
Self-Acceptance, Goodness, Blessings,
Faith, Trust, Love,
Truth, Safety, Freedom,
Peaceful, Harmony, Comfort,
Respect, Redeemer, Joy, Decisive, Mature,
Giver, Confident, Humble, Anointed, Gentle, Meek
Powerful, Healed, Brilliant, Virtuous

Through your positive speaking and thinking help you to realize your potential in a way that also benefits other women, is the ultimate expressing of the power of living, laughing, and loving again. Most importantly, it is through prayer and trusting God in every step of the journey.

STRATEGY SEVEN
ALWAYS PRAY

As I stated in my reflection, prayer is my life-line. It helps me to stay focused and it helps me to communicate with God. I recall a time I was introduced to another form of prayer. I am one of those women that must sleep with the television on. There are times I sleep with headphones while listening to soaking music. I will get to that shortly. However, a program was on and there was a very interesting woman on the Sid Roth Show. It was so profound. I reached for my journal and took pages and pages of notes. I learned something that changed my life forever. She discussed the model of prayer called "soaking prayer" which is quite different from intercessory prayer. She said, "soaking prayer is an act of entering into the presence of God solely to experience His love and His voice." This model was very different from what I've learned and taught others about intercessory prayer. It is passionately advocating, keeping watch, and enforcing God's promises on behalf of others. I know at the time I received this rhema word I knew God was shifting my prayer life to another level. This was another level to defeat spiritual warfare and I know it was to teach others. So, if anyone knows me, I was on a mission to introduce soaking and intercessory prayer along with soaking music as a weapon to defeat the enemy.

For me, this provided a spiritual balance to discern what God was doing and where the enemy's moving next. Soaking prayer was for me and intercessory prayer was for those I was advocating for. The soaking music was to bring about peace and tranquility into my space through both of ways to pray. Soaking Music otherwise known as Soaking Prayer music or Soaking Worship music, is a sub-genre of Christian Music, and is commonly used to denote songs that are used during contemplative prayer in prayer houses and other "soaking" Christian meetings[8]. My favorites, I often listen are Grace Williams and Laura Rhinehart. Both helped during difficult times and brought a sense of peace. I did learn that I have Kingdom authority; therefore, the enemy has no reign or authority over anything. When I realized what a huge mistake I was making in all these years. God took my discernment to another level. At this level, I was very sensitive to what the Holy Spirit wanted me to see, smell, touch, hear, and taste. I was readily armed with spiritual weapons. Very mindful to keep watch from the watchtower discerning who was for me and who was against me. This is critical in this process. Life can be tough, so you can't give up. When you are sober-minded (readily alert and discerning), the enemy cannot seek and devour you (1 Peter 5:8). The following is a prayer to help you get started. However, I have also placed a section in this book of scriptures for your soaking and meditation: **prayers of repentance, prayers of refocus, and prayers of reposition.**

I encourage you to pray this life-changing prayer of continuance wisdom and self-confidence for the next seven days and write down your experience in your journal. Hundreds and I mean hundreds of women through the years of my ministering to women have prayed this prayer and received results:

"Heavenly Father, create in me a clean heart and renew my spirit in righteousness. You formed and fashioned me according to your will and council. I am fearfully and wonderfully made and have been forgiven, made clean and reconciled to you by your grace. I am the temple of your Holy Spirit and you abide in me forever. You have chosen me to be one of your own; because, I was delivered from darkness into your marvelous light. Your scriptures declare that those who reverence you Lord are secure. You are a refuge for me and you surround me with your hedge of protection. Thank you for enabling me to walk in boldness. Your righteousness covers and keeps me from stumbling. The wicked run away when no one is chasing them, but I am not afraid because you are my helper. You declare that I am above and not beneath. I am the head and not the tail and your loving kindness is my shield, in Jesus Name.

You hold me by your right hand my Lord and my God and tell me not to fear; because, you are with me. I have your new mercies each day and you supply me with everything I need for life, peace, and godliness. I am a branch connected to the vine. You are the vine, and I am the branch connected to your life that flows through me. I am part of a chosen generation. I am a special person called a citizen of your holy nation. I am your ambassador. I am a representative in this world. I have faith, gentleness, self-control, and the fruit of the Holy Spirit dwells in me, in Jesus name. I yield each day to my inheritance of your peace, liberty, and glory. In quietness and confidence is my strength. You are for me and more than anything that can come against me.

Father in you is the in-dwelling presence of your Holy Spirit that helps me in any weakness. When I pray, Jesus makes intercession to you on my behalf. I do not place my abilities above your strength because I rely on you. My confidence rests in the knowledge that you are my Helper. So, I have no need to live in fear of any challenge to my mind, body, soul and spirit, in Jesus name. My self-esteem is not diminished. I decree and declare, I have overwhelming victory in my life. That victory is through faith as I love and worship Jesus Christ. I decree and declare, each day I approach you with thanksgiving, praise, worship, prayers, and supplications. I can ask for anything that pleases you and I know that you hear my voice. Thank you for your love, strength, peace, and confidence. You show me every day that I am your daughter and you are my God. And It Is So, In Jesus Name I pray, Amen!"

STRATEGY EIGHT
BELIEVE IT IS SO; LIVE WELL, LIVE BLESSED!

Standing in faith declaring "IT IS SO" is amazing. That means you declaring "yes and amen." It is believing every promise of God will be fulfilled. All the glory belongs to God. When you believe this, it brings joy into your soul. I recall a rainy day caring for my mother. It was a day mother was not feeling well and her spirits were down. It was the day after her chemotherapy so on these days she is usually tired. But, this day was different. Therefore, I knew asking her what was wrong would definitely irritate her, so I would pray, "God give me ideas that would bring mom joy." Later, I was urged (by the Holy Spirit) to get into her bed and watch social media. However, this time I put on YouTube and we would watch various video of all types of genre. Mother loved music and loved to dance. A song by William McDowell entitled "It is so" was in the cue.[9] It had a Caribbean beat and mother loved to dance so the two of us begin to dance. Immediately mother's countenance changed. Out of her spirit she repeated the lyrics:

> Amen, Amen, Amen, Amen
> It is so, it is so
> Amen, Amen, Amen, Amen
> It is so, it is so
> Amen, Amen, Amen, Amen
> It is so, it is so
> Amen, Amen, Amen, Amen
> It is so, it is so

With this praise, mother was stating "it is so" to the will of God and whatever happens, she knows her healing is in effect in Heaven or on earth; either way she is HEALED!!!! I tell you did we danced, we laughed, we danced, we laughed. Immediately, the scripture "the joy of the Lord is our strength (Nehemiah 8:10)" resonated and the atmosphere shifted. We experienced the same encouragement the children of Israel received when Nehemiah encouraged them at the time they were rebuilding the wall. I know you have been working diligently on this self-improvement project. Don't quit! Sooner or later, you'll reach the point where your hard work during in this process will pay off. After Nehemiah and Ezra led their people to rebuild Jerusalem, they had a great day of celebration; just 52 days after the work had begun (Nehemiah, Chapter 8).

Mothers, fathers, grandparents, children, teenagers – everyone - all of them knew how tough life could be. They had a rough past, because of the exile, and their worst days were only a few weeks behind them. Their forefathers had made some choices that cost them dearly. They had known a lot of discouragement, a lot of disappointment - no doubt they were really numb to the entire experience. Likewise, you may be experiencing the same. However, be encouraged and know that life can be tough, but you cannot give up. When you get to a point of total exhaustion, it's hard to keep going. This can be so tough, but you must resolve now to never give up. Don't give up on the patience meter. Don't go dry on the love and laughter well.

IT'S TIME TO SHIFT YOUR PERSPECTIVE

My dear, to live, laugh, and love means you are ready to shift in all areas of your life. You develop the excitement of learning something new. It is stepping outside of your comfort zone and trying something different. It is sitting down and creating a list of everything you love to do, in hopes that you would be able to recognize more elements of those things that are present in your life. You don't have to re-create; because, those elements are already on the inside of you. You just have to shift your perspective get into position and live out your God-given purpose. Personally, I love new experiences, adventure, exploring new people and growing. I created a list some time ago. In a conversation with my mom, I was asked "what do you love about your life?" That question, through me off; because, for once, I could not think of anything. But, mom asked what do you do every day? Cyndy, I challenge you to pay attention to what your life entails and look for the good in it. So, on the next days, while I drove through the city, I listened to audio books to help me grow. I listened to music to give me a sense of calm by singing. I sat in stillness with windows down on those sunny and clear blue-sky days while soaking in Vitamin D. When I stopped to think about these daily moments to appreciate our Creator and His creations, the shift made a big difference in my outlook on life.

It's time to shift! Start applying this action to every area of life and watch how the little changes work together to make one big exponential change in your life. It's what one of my mentees Cristen calls "The Big Good." Meaning, God rewards us in the core areas of our life: spiritual, emotional, relationships, career, finance, education, and physical on another level. It is fulfillment in every area of your life, no area lacking; because, you focused on another area. It can become tiring and often physically impossible to pursue a "Big Good," totally fulfilled life by one's self. This is why we need and must trust God. Believing all things are possible (Luke 1:37) to make the best of tough situations and get through them. I asked her to go deeper in her thinking and tell me more. Little did she know, she was confirming what I had been asking God all week for this guidebook. Cristen went on to share that as we work toward building this "Big Good" or this ideal life, we will inevitably encounter times when we want nothing more than to press fast forward and step ahead to have better things and receive what we have been praying God for. Is this your thought too?

Unfortunately, as I shared with her and you too my dear this is not reality. You must be careful of this thought. It provides the temptation of giving up, throwing in the towel, walking way, or compromising who you are. I want you to take a moment, breathe, and self-reflect. By shifting your perspective, you can find a deeper purpose to motivate you. I often say: when you fall in love with the process of self-reflection, you will always have a clear understanding of who's in control, and then everything in your life will seem easy. I read a quote by Jean Shinoda Bolen, "When you recover or discover something that nourishes your soul and brings joy, care enough about yourself to make room for it in your life."[10]

It is developing a lifestyle of virtue by cherishing every moment and living life to the fullest (Ephesians 3:20, Amp.). God has granted you access to live, laugh, and love. This access provides you the privilege to live out every moment of your life. By living every moment, you are aware of who you are, where you are, what you are doing, what you want, what you don't want, go where you are celebrated and not tolerated. It is making informed choices on a moment by moment basis. At this level of your change, two things are important: forget the past and keep your eyes on the goal ahead (Philippians 3:12, NIV). This ability allows you to live your life without regrets. I discovered during this process that many of the so-called truths I was raised with and forced to believe were not truths at all. So, I have adopted from Jairek Robbins[9] along my own truth or T.R.U.T.H. that I can share with you:

🌑 WISDOM KEY APPLICATION

T – You must have a clear and defined **trajectory** of how you are going to live, laugh, and love.

R – You have to be willing to **rebuke** the Sanballat and Tabias (nayslayers), **renounce** their doubts, and be **relentless** in your approach to your new life (Nehemiah 2:10)

U- You have to be **unconventional** with your strategies, **unified** in your thoughts and beliefs (Philippians 2:5).

T – You will need a massive amount of **tenacity** to stand against the adversities that come at you (Ephesians 6:10).

H – You will need create a safe **haven** and you will need to develop daily **habits** to help your mind, body and spirit remain **healthy**, so you can live, laugh, and love (3 John 1:2).

EXERCISE: I want you to take each of the 12-Steps in recovery for physical, emotional, or sexual abuse issues and journal for the next 12 months (Appendix III). Each month will be your focus to keep you intentional in maintaining your healing. Make sure you write them down and date them as well.

Here is an example of application of this exercise:

> • **STEP ONE** We admit we are powerless over the past, and as a result, our lives have become unmanageable

> • What can you do each day to apply the **T.R.U.T.H.** formula to your life and business from what you have learned from Step One? Remember, I cannot do everything. Incorporate the women God has assigned to help me in my vision. Utilize my tribe to provide wisdom on elements of my business and life I do not understand.

> • What are the daily habits and personal rituals you can use to keep yourself focused and on track from Step One? Beginning my day with prayer and worship. Review my agenda for the day and make sure I follow the plan for each day.

FINAL WORDS OF REFLECTION

Our journey together is coming to a close my dear. I want you to remember to focus on more than just yourself, you are in your purpose. You have gained your strength, so now you are equipped to go and help others. Prayerfully, you are clear, and you are no longer spending time on your challenges, but you are spending your time on achieving the results you are after on a daily basis. It is going to take the power of prayer, meditation, and activation to get things done. No more procrastination. No more excuses. As we affectionately say in the south, no more wouldda, couldda, shouldda. And one of my favorites, fixing to and "finna" (this is a Southern thing).

Regardless of what stage you are in the process, it is my prayer after reading this chapter, you have a much better understanding of the incredible results you can achieve through the strategies learned from each exercise. I pray they have been helpful, and you now have a clear plan of action to live, laugh, and love.

I hope this guidebook has helped you to raise your level of expectation and that you will not lower your standards under any circumstances. Oprah Winfrey has been quoted saying, "it isn't until you come to a spiritual understanding of who you are – not necessarily a religious feeling, but deep down, the spirit within – that you can begin to take control." She goes on to express, "Often, we don't even realize who we're meant to be; because, we're so busy trying to live out someone else's ideas. But other people and their opinions hold no power in defining our destiny." At the end of the day, I hope and pray you will accept this challenge, and focus on what's important. Don't allow your emotions to get in the way. Accept the reality of your current situation. Be careful of your words, pray, and believe. To take all this you learn to really live, laugh, and love by giving your best efforts every day. Please share what you have learned; because, when you spend more time giving back you will find your purposeful life will be closer than you can ever ask, think, or imagine (Ephesians 3:20). I end with this my dear, I am so proud of you. You are AMAZING!!! "You took a risk of faith, and now you are healed and whole. Live Well, Live Blessed (Mark 5:34, MSG)!!! Doves Love to you and big hugs!!!

NOTES

1. Patterson, C.A. (2015). Let go, move on (ch. 1) In C. Patterson, My life matters: A guide to creating a mentor relationship that effectively ministers to the heart of your mentee and causes their authentic transformation. Houston, TX: Seeds of Love Publishing

2. Calhoun, A. A., (2005). Spiritual exercises focusing on God and self (ch. 7) In A. Calhoun, Spiritual disciplines handbook: Practices that transform us.

3. American Counseling Association (2014). ACA code of ethics: C.2. Professional Competence. Alexandria VA.

4. Eivaz, J.(2016). Introduction (pg. 13). In J. Eivaz, The intercessors handbook: how to pray with boldness, authority and supernatural power.

5. Marshall, D. (2015). Move Out of Your Own Way: 10 Steps to Stop Self-Sabotage.

6. Chan, S., (1998). The discernment of spirits (ch. 11) In S. Chan, Spiritual theology: A systematic study of the Christian life. Downers Grove, IL: InterVarsity Press.

7. Patterson, C.A. (2011). It Had to Happen: Understanding everything you go through in life is for God's purpose. Houston, TX: Seeds of Love Publishing.

8. Wikipedia contributors. "Soaking music." Wikipedia, The Free Encyclopedia. Wikipedia, The Free Encyclopedia, 14 Nov. 2016. Web. 12 Feb. 2018.

9. William McDowell - It Is So feat. Travis Greene (OFFICIAL VIDEO) https://www.youtube.com/watch?v=PlfO6baiVUw

10. Robins, J. (2014). Live It!: Achieve Success by Living with Purpose. Grand Harbor Press. ISBN 147782474X.

APPENDIX I

Flush Out Those False Beliefs!

Step 1

Do you ever feel stuck in a rut of unhelpful beliefs, leading to unhealthy habits causing unconscious actions? This checklist may give you an idea of what beliefs need updating!

When under pressure I _____
_____.

I often feel guilty about _____
_____.

When _____ happens I stress out and feel like_____
_____.

My *Achilles'* heel (greatest weakness) is _____
_____.

I am always trying to stop _____
_____ from happening.

When the unexpected happens I _____
_____.

I always try to _____
_____.

The biggest obstacle that stops me loving and approving of myself is ____
_____.

What drives most of my behavior is _____

_____.

I am afraid of _____

_____.

I seek my _____'s approval (always/mostly/
usually/occasionally)

My most frequent negative and uncomfortable emotion is
feeling _____

_____.

The feeling I dislike the most is _____

_____.

I need to learn to _____

_____.

Congratulations, that took courage!

Step 2

Now you have identified your false beliefs, go back and re-do the
exercise in your journal writing how you would like to be.

For example: When under pressure I. . . panic to When under pressure I … think about the situation calmly and ask for support.

APPENDIX II

LIFE STRESS TEST

As women, we are often stressed and don't know why. Without realizing the effects that life circumstances have on us, we tend to sweep our feelings of frustration, sadness, and turmoil under the rug. In the past 12 to 24 months, which of the following major life events have taken place in your life?

Fill in the points for each event that you have experienced this year. When you're done looking at the whole list, add up the points for each event and check your score at the bottom.

1. Death of Spouse (100 points)

2. Divorce (73 points)

3. Marital or Relationship Partner separation (65 points)

4. Jail term (64 points)

5. Death of close family member (63 points)

6. Personal Injury or illness (53 points)

7. Marriage (50 points)

8. Fired from work (47 points)

☐ 9. Marital or Relationship Partner reconciliation (45 points)

☐ 10. Retirement (45 points)

☐ 11. Change in family member's health (44 points)

☐ 12. Pregnancy (40 points)

☐ 13. Sex difficulties (39 points)

☐ 14. Addition to family (39 points)

☐ 15. Business readjustment (39 points)

☐ 16. Change in financial status (38 points)

☐ 17. Death of close friend (37 points)

☐ 18. Change to a different line of work (36 points)

☐ 19. Change in number of marital/relationship arguments (35 points)

☐ 20. Mortgage or loan over $30,000 (31 points)

☐ 21. Foreclosure of mortgage or loan (30 points)

☐ 22. Change in work responsibilities (29 points)

☐ 23. Trouble with in-laws (29 points)

☐ 24. Outstanding personal achievement (28 points)

☐ 25. Spouse begins or stops work (26 points)

☐ 26. Starting or finishing school (26 points)

☐ 27. Change in living conditions (25 points)

☐ 28. Revision of personal habits (24 points)

☐ 29. Trouble with boss (23 points)

☐ 30. Change is work hours/conditions (20 points)

☐ 31. Change in residence (20 points)

☐ 32. Change in schools (20 points)

☐ 33. Change in recreational habits (19 points)

☐ 34. Change in church activities (19 points)

☐ 35. Change in social activities (18 points)

☐ 36. Mortgage or loan under $20,000 (17 points)

☐ 37. Change in sleeping habits (16 points)

☐ 38. Change in number of family gatherings (15 points)

☐ 39. Change in eating habits (15 points)

☐ 40. Vacation (13 points)

☐ 41. Christmas season (12 points)

☐ 42. Minor violations of the law (11 points)

☐ Your Total Score

This scale shows the kind of life pressure that you are facing. Depending on your coping skills or the lack thereof, this scale can predict the likelihood that you will fall victim to a stress related illness. The illness could be mild - frequent tension headaches, acid indigestion, and/or loss of sleep to very serious illness like ulcers, cancer, migraines, and the like.

LIFE STRESS SCORES

0-149: Low susceptibility to stress-related illness.

150-299: Medium susceptibility to stress-related illness: Learn and practice relaxation and stress management skills and a healthy well life style.

300 and over: High susceptibility to stress-related illness: Daily practice of relaxation skills is very important for your wellness. Take care of it now before a serious illness erupts or an affliction becomes worse.

Permission to reprint the Life Stress Test received from: Dr. Tim Lowenstein
P.O. Box 127 Port Angeles, WA 98362 **www.stressmarket.com**

APPENDIX III

12 Steps: Physical / Emotional and Sexual Abuse

STEP ONE We admit we are powerless over the past, and as a result, our lives have become unmanageable.

STEP TWO Believe God can restore us to wholeness, and realize this power can always be trusted to bring healing and wholeness in our lives.

STEP THREE Make a decision to turn our lives and our wills to the care of God, realizing we have not always understood His unconditional love. Choose to believe He does love us, is worthy of trust, and will help us to understand Him as we seek His truth.

STEP FOUR Make a searching and fearless moral inventory of ourselves, realizing all wrongs can be forgiven. Renounce the lie that the abuse was our fault.

STEP FIVE Admit to God, to ourselves, and to another human being, the exact nature of the wrongs in our lives. This will include those acts perpetrated against us, as well as those wrongs we perpetrated against others.

STEP SIX By accepting God's cleansing, we can renounce our shame. Now we are ready to have God remove all these character distortions and defects.

STEP SEVEN Humbly ask Him to remove our short-comings, including our guilt. We release our fear and submit to Him.

STEP EIGHT Make a list of all persons who have harmed us and become willing to seek God's help in forgiving our perpetrators, as well as forgiving ourselves. Realize we've also harmed others and become willing to make amends to them.

STEP NINE Extend forgiveness to ourselves and to others who have perpetrated against us, realizing this is an attitude of the heart, not always confrontation. Make direct amends, asking forgiveness from those people we have harmed, except when to do so would injure them or others.

STEP TEN Continue to take personal inventory as new memories and issues surface. We continue to renounce our shame and guilt, but when we are wrong, promptly admit it.

STEP ELEVEN Continue to seek God through prayer and meditation to improve our understanding of His character. Praying for knowledge of His truth in our lives, His will for us, and for the power to carry that out.

STEP TWELVE Having a spiritual awakening as we accept God's love and healing through these steps, we try to carry His message of hope to others. Practice these principles as new memories and issues surface, claiming God's promise of restoration and wholeness.

Celebrate Recovery (2009). Retrieved from www.celebraterecovery.com

PRAYERS OF REPENTANCE, REFOCUS, AND REPOSITION

PRAYER SCRIPTURES OF REPENTANCE

PSALM 51:10

Create in me a clean heart, O God. Renew a loyal spirit within me.

PSALM 32:5

Finally, I confessed all my sins to you and stopped trying to hide my guilt. I said to myself, "I will confess my rebellion to the Lord." And you forgave me! All my guilt is gone.

PSALM 24:10

Who is the King of glory? The Lord of Heaven's Armies— he is the King of glory.

JOB 34:32

For 'I don't know what evil I have done—tell me. If I have done wrong, I will stop at once'?

PSALM 42:8

But each day the Lord pours his unfailing love upon me, and through each night I sing his songs, praying to God who gives me life.

PSALM 19:12-14

How can I know all the sins lurking in my heart? Cleanse me from these hidden faults. 13 Keep your servant from deliberate sins! Don't let them control me. Then I will be free of guilt and innocent of great sin.

PSALM 32:5

Finally, I confessed all my sins to you and stopped trying to hide my guilt. I said to myself, "I will confess my rebellion to the Lord." And you forgave me! All my guilt is gone.

PRAYER SCRIPTURES TO HELP YOU REFOCUS

JOB 42:1-6 (MESSAGE BIBLE)

"I'm convinced: You can do anything and everything. Nothing and no one can upset your plans. You asked, 'Who is this muddying the water, ignorantly confusing the issue, second-guessing my purposes?' I admit it. I was the one. I babbled on about things far beyond me, made small talk about wonders way over my head. You told me, 'Listen, and let me do the talking. Let me ask the questions. You give the answers.' I admit I once lived by rumors of you; now I have it all firsthand—from my own eyes and ears! I'm sorry—forgive me. I'll never do that again, I promise! I'll never again live on crusts of hearsay, crumbs of rumor."

PHILIPPIANS 3:13-14

13 I focus on this one thing: Forgetting the past and looking forward to what lies ahead, 14 I press on to reach the end of the race and receive the heavenly prize for which God, through Christ Jesus, is calling us.

PSALM 62:5-7, 9 (MESSAGE BIBLE)

6 Everything I hope for comes from him, so why not? He's solid rock under my feet, breathing room for my soul, An impregnable castle: I'm set for life. 7-9 My help and glory are in God – granite-strength and safe-harbor-God– Man as such is smoke, woman as such, a mirage. Put them together, they're nothing; two times nothing is nothing.

EXODUS 15:2

The Lord is my strength and my song; he has given me victory. This is my God, and I will praise him– my father's God, and I will exalt him!

PSALM 121:1-2

1 I look up to the mountains– does my help come from there?2 My help comes from the Lord, who made heaven and earth!

PRAYER SCRIPTURES TO HELP YOU REPOSITION

PSALM 26:2

Now I stand on solid ground, and I will publicly praise the Lord.

EXODUS 33:13

If it is true that you look favorably on me, let me know your ways so I may understand you more fully and continue to enjoy your favor. And remember that this nation is your very own people."

PSALM 86:11

Teach me your ways, O Lord, that I may live according to your truth! Grant me purity of heart, so that I may honor you.

PSALM 143:8-10

Let me hear of your unfailing love each morning, for I am trusting you. Show me where to walk, for I give myself to you. 9 Rescue me from my enemies, Lord; I run to you to hide me. 10 Teach me to do your will, for you are my God. May your gracious Spirit lead me forward on a firm footing.

PSALM 73:24

You guide me with your counsel, leading me to a glorious destiny.

PSALM 25:4-5

4 Show me the right path, O Lord; point out the road for me to follow. 5 Lead me by your truth and teach me, for you are the God who saves me. All day long I put my hope in you.

SUGGESTIONS FOR WOMEN WHO CHOOSE TO FORM AN ACCOUNTABILITY GROUP OUT OF THIS BOOK.

1. Accountability partners are keys in your life in becoming better.

2. Come to the group prepared and prayed up. You will find that careful preparation will greatly enrich your time spent in group discussion.

3. Be willing to participate in the discussion. Encouraging each other in the group to discuss what you discovered about your-self. Always stick to the topic being discussed.

4. Be sensitive to the others in the group. Listen attentively to each other's testimony. You may be surprised by their insights!

5. Remember that anything said in the group is confidential and should not be discussed outside of your group unless specific permission is given to do so.

OTHER WORKS BY

CYNTHIA A. PATTERSON

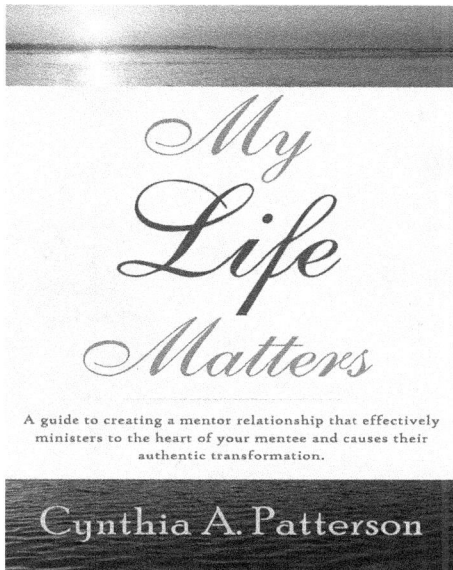

My Life Matters

A guide to creating a mentor relationship that effectively ministers to the heart of your mentee and causes their authentic transformation.

Cynthia A. Patterson

A guide to creating a mentor relationship that effectively ministers to the heart of your mentee and causes their authentic transformation

Are you in need of a mentor? Do you have trouble connecting with other women? Do you feel the tug at your heart to mentor women, but you feel inadequate? My Life Matters is a book written with you in mind. You will:

- Gain clarity about your purpose

- Get critical information about what it takes to connect authentically with other women

- Get to see what goes on in the hearts and minds of real women and learn about their needs and what sparked their transformations.

Powerful testimonies from real women are in the beginning of each chapter, along with powerful parallels to the ultimate biblical female mentor relationship, Ruth and Naomi.

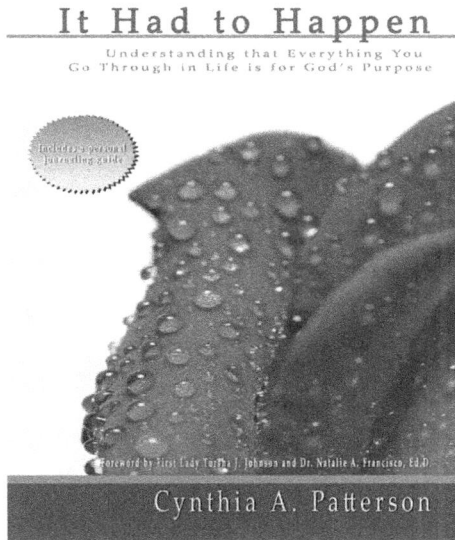

It Had to Happen
Understanding that Everything You
Go Through in Life is for God's Purpose

Cynthia A. Patterson

*Understanding that Everything You Go Through in Life is
for God's Purpose*

It Had to Happen is an inspiring book that will heal wounds,
restore your faith and dramatically change your relationship with
God. After carefully retracing your steps, you will be able to identify with the direction you are heading and begin your journey with
confidence and faith. During this process, you'll learn:

- The secrets needed to pursue your purpose.

- To enjoy the success of finding out who you really are.

And most importantly, understand that past mistakes simply,
HAD TO HAPPEN!

It Had to Happen is available on Amazon, Barnes & Noble and
other online book stores.

Live **BETTER** Everyday

Believing Every Trial and Tribulation Eventually Reverses

Cynthia A. Patterson

4-Weeks of Prayer and Inspiration to help you live

Believing Every Trial and Tribulation Eventually Reverses

Are you sick and tired of being sick and tired? Do you feel like your life is stuck? Are you held back by past challenges or pain?

Live Better Everyday will inspire you to let your dreams rise to new heights as a world of possibilities waits to be discovered. Be inspired and encouraged through prayers, reflections, and affirmations to better your hopes and plans for the future. Wherever you may have been and whatever you may have done, you will Live BETTER Everyday!

ABOUT THE AUTHOR

CYNTHIA A. PATTERSON is a transformational leader and life coach specializing in spiritual growth development and empowerment. She has been called a 21st Century Abolitionist who coach women that desperately want to liberate themselves from past hurts and pain. She shows them how to spiritually heal so they can awaken their deepest desires and live their greatest dreams.

A sought-after inspirational speaker who has a genuine passion to inspire and encourage women. She is known for her amazing, approachable, engaging, and transparent style. Her deep passion is obvious as she takes her audience on a journey. Her wisdom is shared with loads of practical advice and application. No matter what the topic, her passion and prayer is that every woman or teenage girl duplicates and leaves inspired.

Cynthia holds a Masters' in Christian Counseling of Substance Abuse and Addictive Disorders, Bachelor in Christian Leadership Development, Ordained and Licensed Minister, Certified Pastoral Counselor, Certified Christian Life Coach, Certified International Recovery Coach and Trainer, Certified Drug Education Instructor & Trainer, and Certified Domestic Violence Trauma Specialist. Currently pursuing a Doctor of Education in Organizational Leadership and Behavioral Health.

Cynthia loves to laugh and loves helping and serving God's daughters. She has been ministering to women and girls for nearly 25 years.

CONTACT INFORMATION

Join Cynthia in her movement to minister the Gospel of Jesus Christ to women of all social classes. She speaks on topics such as:

This Girl is on Fire!

What's Your Problem?

When it doesn't get better, but worse

Don't Give up!

Becoming a Woman of Wisdom

Living Your Best Life!

Single for a Season

…and so much more!

If you wish for Cynthia to come and speak at your women's conferences, workshops, seminars, retreat, group coaching, corporate leadership conferences, please request via email at info@doveslove.org. Stay connected with Cynthia through social media:

Website: www.iamcynthiapatterson.com

Ministry Website: www.doveslove.org

Facebook: https://www.facebook.com/doveministryinc

Twitter: www.twitter.com/cyndypatterson

Instagram: www.instagram.com/cynthiapatterson

www.ingramcontent.com/pod-product-compliance
Lightning Source LLC
Chambersburg PA
CBHW020944090426
42736CB00010B/1249